Conroy Maddox

SALVADOR DALÍ
1904–1989

Eccentric and Genius

Benedikt Taschen

Front cover:
The Chemist of Ampurdan Looking for Absolutely Nothing, 1936
Le pharmacien de l'Ampurdan ne cherchant absolument rien
Oil on wood, 30 × 52 cm
Folkwang Museum, Essen

Frontispiece:
**Dream Caused by the Flight of a Bee around a Pomegranate,
a Second before Waking Up, 1944**
*Rêve causé pa le vol d'une abeille autour d'une pomme-grenade
une seconde avant l'éveil*
Oil on canvas, 51 × 41 cm
Thyssen-Bornemisza Collection, Lugano-Castagnola

© The Hamlyn Publishing Group Ltd., 1979;
Newnes Books, 1983
© 1990 Benedikt Taschen Verlag GmbH
Hohenzollernring 53, D-5000 Köln 1
© for the illustrations: VG Bild-Kunst, Bonn
Editor: Angelika Muthesius, Cologne
Cover design: Peter Feierabend, Berlin
Printed in Germany
ISBN 3-8228-0289-1
GB

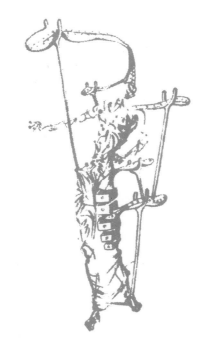

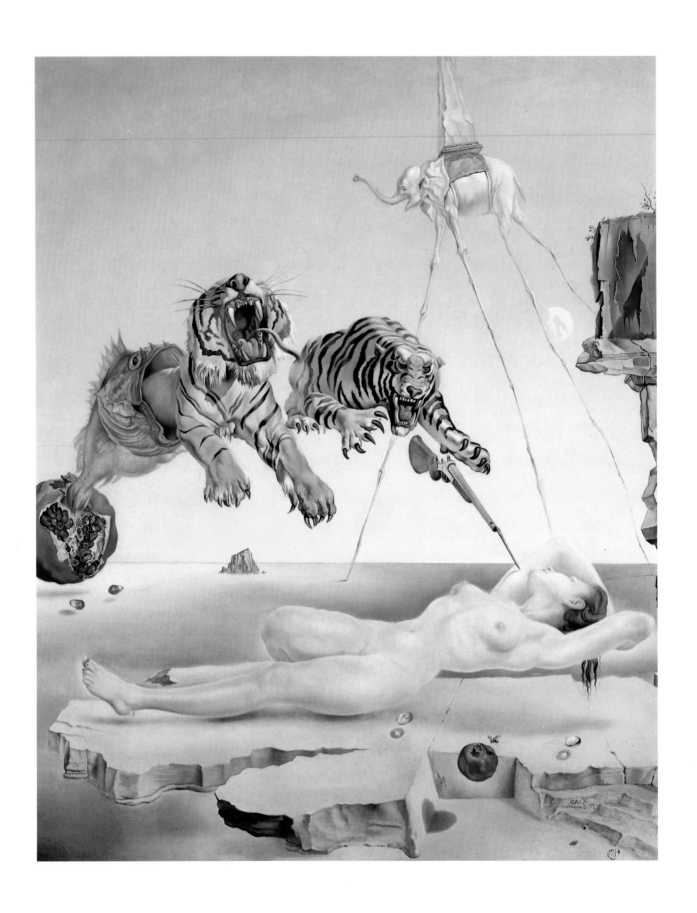

Contents

Introduction

Whatever the future judgement of Salvador Dalí may be, it cannot be denied that he has a place all his own in the history of modern art. His fame has been an issue of controversy, kept alive as much by Dalí's own provocative exhibitionism as by the critics and press, who have so consistently condemned him for his excesses: the words 'neurotic', 'egocentric' and 'mad' are frequently used when referring to him. Over the years he has become so closely identified with Surrealism that it is possible to say that in the public mind Surrealism simply is Salvador Dalí. Considering the publicity there is some excuse for this prevalent error.

Whatever his influence has been on the art of the 20th century, few can deny the importance of his contribution. In fact, it could be argued that it is as great as that of his famous fellow-countryman, Picasso. Dalí himself said: 'Picasso is perhaps a minor painter, but he is the most destructive genius of modern times.' Certainly the revelatory nature of Dalí's imagery between 1929 and 1939 was the most potent of our age, which makes it that much more difficult to assess its aesthetic worth. From early childhood he was abnormally imaginative, selfishly preoccupied with his own pleasures, cynically parading his audacity and his perverse violence. In his book *Surrealism* Julien Levy sees him as 'a man who bears the stigma of the Spanish Inquisition, the sexual ecstasies of Spain's mystics . . .' and we have only to explore the iconography of his work to affirm the connection with that Spanish heritage.

If the problem is correctly stated, then Dalí, though not alone in the field, is perhaps the first to have consistently exploited the findings of Freud and psychoanalysis and to have deliberately insisted on the right of man to his own madness. His development of a 'paranoid-critical' approach, which is so strikingly apparant in all aspects of his thought, was one of the most revolutionary contributions to Surrealism and was the touchstone which gave Dalí's work its unique character and dominated his evolution as an artist. As early as 1920 André Breton, who was to play such an important part in the Surrealist movement, had proposed 'allegiance to folly, to dreams, to the incoherent, to the hyperbolic – in a word to all that is contrary to the general appearance of reality'. Several years were to go by before Dalí played his pictorial and critical part; it is necessary, therefore, to trace his development and the influences that were to have such a crucial effect on what he was to call his images of 'concrete irrationality'.

"The two greatest strokes of luck that can happen to a painter are (1) to be Spanish, (2) to be called Dalí."
Salvador Dalí

The Burning Giraffe, 1936/37
Girafe en feu
Oil on canvas, 35 x 27 cm
Emanuel Hoffmann Collection,
Kunstmuseum, Basle

Biography

Salvador Dalí was born at 8.45 on the morning of 11th May 1904, in the Spanish town of Figueras, where his father was a notary and a man of some local importance. The name Salvador had originally been given to his brother who had died three years before Dalí was born. An only child until his sister Ana María arrived, he was thoroughly spoilt and allowed to do almost anything he pleased. In his autobiography, Dalí gives a vivid account of these early years: 'My brother and I resembled each other like two drops of water, but we had different reflections. Like myself he had the unmistakeable facial morphology of a genius. He gave signs of alarming precocity, but his glance was veiled by a melancholy characteristic insurmountable intelligence. I, on the other hand, was much less intelligent but I reflected everything. I was to become the prototype *par excellence* of the phenomenally retarded "polymorphous pervert" having kept intact all the reminiscences of the nursling's erogenous paradises; I clutched at pleasure with boundless, selfish eagerness and at the slightest provocation I would become dangerous.'[1] He does not neglect to record other memories, such as his intra-uterine life 'as though it were yesterday'; he identifies it as paradise, and also the colour of hell, but soft, warm and immobile. One of his pre-birth visions, he tells us, was that of a pair of eggs sizzling in a pan – but without the pan – 'an ever-hallucinatory image' which he could later reproduce at will.

His education began in a local school and then in the Academy in Figueras, run by the Brothers of the Marist Order. To his parents' dismay he was a poor pupil. A desire to do the exact opposite of what everyone else did assumed immense importance in his eyes, and hours were spent dreaming up the most anti-social acts in order to astonish his schoolmates. Many revealed themselves in acts of aggression. Walking with a young boy one day, he pushed him over a bridge on to the rocks some fifteen feet below, and then spent the afternoon eating cherries in a rocking chair as he watched the blood-stained basins being brought from the bedroom. Alone with his three-year-old sister, he dealt her a terrible kick on the head, which gave him a 'delirious joy'. He was given a wounded bat one day and took it to his hiding place in a wash-house. Next morning it lay, half dead, covered with frenzied ants. Overcome with emotion, he bit into the writhing mass. He also took an inexplicable pleasure in throwing himself down steps. The pain was insignificant, the intense joy was overwhelming, and he repeated the performance many times, perfectly

Satirical drawing, 1920
Ink on card
Enrique Sabater Collection

This work, a gift to his uncle, was one of the earliest Dalís known to us.

Woman with Rose Head, 1935
Femme à tête de roses
Oil on board, 35 x 27 cm
Kunsthaus, Zurich

9

aware of the effect it produced on his fellow pupils. On another occasion he smashed a boy's violin to prove that painting was superior to music.

Before Dalí was six years old, he was showing considerable talent as an artist. Fleur Cowles in her book on Dalí reproduces the earliest known work, a landscape painted postcard-size. It was followed by two much more ambitious works, *Portrait of Helen of Troy* and *Joseph Greeting his Brethren,* executed in the precise 19th-century literary style. For a studio, Dalí was given the use of an old wash-house at the top of the house. On hot days he would fill a tub full of water, remove his clothes and sit in it for hours, painting. Pinned to the walls around were his pictures, painted on the covers of hat boxes taken from his aunt's millinery shop, as well as reproductions of the Renaissance masters torn from magazines. There he found refuge, and the solitude that he always so desperately sought. To be alone became a mania, and all kinds of excuses were found which would permit him to rush upstairs to the laundry. Here he felt unique, living out his fantasies, playing at being a genius: 'If you play at being a genius, you become one.'

He was at the mercy of delirious egocentricity. His parents, not

Cadaqués, 1923
Oil on canvas, 96.5 x 127 cm
Collection of
Mr and Mrs A. Reynolds Morse,
Salvador Dalí Museum,
St. Petersburg (Florida)

Cadaqués is a small fishing village where Dalí spent his summers while still a student.

unaware of his growing artistic ability, sent him to a friend of theirs in the country. Ramón Pitchot was a rich connoisseur of art and a gifted painter in the Impressionist manner. It was a considerably talented family. Two sons were musicians, one of the daughters was an opera singer and another was married to a Spanish poet. Their estate was known as the Muli de la Torre (The Tower Mill). Dalí's period with this family was to have an important influence on his life and illuminates many of the erotic fantasies that were to appear in later works.

Although the practical side of the mill had little interest, the tower produced a powerful effect on his imagination. It became a 'sacred spot', the very centre of his world. Each day he would have his meals in a room hung with the many Impressionist paintings of Ramón Pitchot. To the young Dalí these 'visual cocktails' with their brilliant decorative unity were an endless fascination. It was not long before he was deeply committed to this new and exciting way of looking at nature. 'It represented,' he tells us, 'my first contact with an anti-academic and revolutionary aesthetic theory.'

Pitchot provided him with a large whitewashed room as a studio where, consumed by a creative fever, he explored the instantaneous luminosity that he found so tantalising in these new paintings. On one occasion, having used up all his canvas, he decided to utilise an old wooden door, somewhat worm-eaten, for a subject that had been in his mind for some time, a still-life of a large bunch of cherries. They were to be painted in three colours only and applied directly from the tube. Setting up an

Figure between the Rocks, 1926
Personnage parmi les roches
Oil on plywood, 27 x 41 cm
Collection of
Mr and Mrs A. Reynolds Morse,
Salvador Dalí Museum,
St. Petersburg (Florida)

"When I was three, I wanted to be a cook. At the age of six I wanted to be Napoleon. Since then my ambition has increased all the time."
Salvador Dalí

11

Apparatus and Hand, 1927
Appareil et main
Oil on panel, 62 x 48 cm
Collection of
Mr and Mrs A. Reynolds Morse,
Salvador Dalí Museum,
St. Petersburg, Florida

This work is beginning to show evidence of his growing hallucinatory power.

immense pile of cherries as a model, he attacked the wooden surface. Soon he found that he was painting to the rhythm of the mill, each cherry being realised with three touches of colours – vermilion for the lighter side, carmine for the shade, white for the highlight. The whole effect, with the thick daubs of colour, assumed an astonishing realism. Completely engrossed in keeping up with the sound of the mill, he discovered that he had forgotten to add the stems. 'Suddenly, I had an idea. I took a handful of cherries and began to eat them. As soon as one of them was swallowed, I would glue the stem directly to my painting in the appropriate place.' The gluing on of cherry stems produced an unforeseen effect of startling 'finish'. To further reinforce the realism, he then proceeded to introduce real worms into the wormholes, which looked as though they belonged to the painted cherries. It must have been an impressive work. Pitchot, who turned up at that moment, was heard to mutter, 'That shows genius.'

Needless to say, Dalı had his rituals at the Tower Mill. Waking in the morning he went through an exhibitionist fantasy with the maid. At breakfast, because he liked the sensation, he poured hot milk and coffee down his chest, then went to the studio to paint. Here, he tells us, he worked on 'pictorial inventions, re-inventions of Impressionism, the reaffirmation and rebirth of my aesthetic megalomania'.

Before Dalí left the Pitchots' there was a notable incident dominated by an object that was to find its way into his gallery of recurrent images. At the time of the linden blossom picking, helping to fetch the ladders from the tower attic, he discovered a heavy metal crown, used for some theatrical production, and an old crutch. It was an exciting find, loaded with fetishist significance. Among the blossom pickers was an extremely attractive woman with large breasts, accompanied by her twelve-year-old daughter. Dalí instantly fell in love with the girl, identifying her with all his false memories of the ideal woman. Finding that his impulsive behaviour only succeeded in frightening the young girl, he found solace in covertly watching the mother, in particular her large firm breasts, beneath which he had a voluptuous desire to rest the upper bifurcate part of the crutch he had discovered.

Overcome with longing, he invented a ruse which could fulfil the fantasy. Finding a closed area lit only by a small window overlooking the garden, his attention was drawn to three melons hanging from the rafters. They suggested to his feverish mind a substitute even more desirable than the woman's breasts. Carefully entangling his diabolo in the vines that grew on the outside wall above the window, he then asked the blossom picker to retrieve the toy. While she moved the ladder to the desired spot, he rushed back to the room, stripped off his clothes, placed the crown on his head and covered himself with an ermine cloak. At the exact moment the upper part of the woman's body filled the small window space, he let slip the cloak from his naked body and gently placed the crutch beneath the lower part of one of the ripening melons, pressing it into the soft fruit. His gaze wandered back and forth between the swollen breasts and the melon. Under the persistent pressure, the melon began to drip, covering him with its sweet and sticky juice.

Further pressure detached the melon, which fell on to his head at the exact moment the woman, having disentangled the diabolo, descended the ladder. Hurriedly throwing himself on the floor he lay breathless, waiting, unsuccessfully, to be discovered. He was trembling with exhaustion; the two remaining melons appeared as a 'sinister symbol and no longer evoked the beautiful blossom-gatherer's two breasts, sunny with

Page 14:
The Lugubrious Game, 1929
Le jeu lugubre
Oil and collage on canvas,
44.4 x 30.3 cm
Claude Hersaint Collection, Paris

The first truly Surrealist painting by Dalí. The scatological elements were of some concern to the Surrealists when they first saw this work.

Page 15:
The First Days of Spring, 1929
Les premiers jours du printemps
Oil on board with collage,
49.5 x 64 cm
Private collection, Paris

Dalí's working method during this period was to adapt the Surrealist processes of automatic writing to painting, of trying to see 'like a medium' the images that would appear in his imagination.

Illumined Pleasures, 1929
Les plaisirs illuminés
Oil and collage on composition
board, 23.8 x 34.5 cm
The Sidney and Harriet Janis
Collection,
Gift to the Museum of Modern Art,
New York

Although part of this picture is composed of collage, the skilfully painted areas create confusion about what is paint and what is photography. Dalí's debt to de Chirico is revealed in the pictures within the picture as well as in the emotive use of perspective. Other influences derive from Max Ernst (the bird totem on the left of the centre box) and Magritte (the painted cyclists on the right). In a number of early works, he pasted down line engravings and photographs which were then faithfully copied so as to be indistinguishable from the original, as in another painting, *Accommodations of Desire* of 1929 (p. 17).

afternoon. Instead, they too now seemed to stir like two dead things rolled into balls, like two petrified hedgehogs.' The secret pleasure Dalí derived from that crutch remained with him throughout, not only as a fetish in erotic acts, but as a predominant image in many obsessive and fanciful ways in his paintings. Later he was to conceive the idea of a tiny facial crutch to be worn by 'criminally elegant women', so that they could experience 'the sacred tug of exhibitionism encrusted in the flesh of their own faces'.

Encouraged by Pitchot, Dalí's father enrolled him in Señor Nuñez's art classes in Figueras. Nuñez appears to have been a congenial teacher. Perhaps he sensed something of the later brilliance in his eccentric but dedicated pupil. Stimulated by the individual attention he received, Dalí was soon reviving his passion for the great masters of the Renaissance and exploring the mysteries of chiaroscuro. Reading also began to be an obsession, with philosophy as his favourite subject. Nietzsche's *Thus Spake Zarathustra* and Voltaire's *Philosophical Dictionary* became firm favourites. His real joy was Kant, whom he read and re-read without understanding a word: 'such an important and useless book'. He dipped into Spinoza, and then turned to Descartes, on whom he was to base much of his later research. His paintings were now beginning to attract attention, and invitations to show in regional exhibitions followed.

In the meantime, secondary studies continued at the Marist School, although most of the teachers had given up any hope of teaching him anything. Nose-bleeding and 'angina' became regular means of avoiding the hateful lessons. Frantically he awaited vacation time, which was always spent in the village of Cadaqués on the Mediterranean coast. The rocks and beaches which he came to know so well in his solitary wanderings became the very spot which he adored with a 'fanatical fidelity' and which he thought the most beautiful landscape in the world, with rocky contours that only Leonardo could have captured. It was to affect his vision profoundly: those strangely coloured rocks and deserted beaches are faithfully imprinted and appear in many studies with extraordinary love and clarity. Dalí made the geological phenomena of Catalonia very much his own.

Although the family had little faith in his earning a living by art, they realised the futility of trying to change their young son's mind. A compromise was proposed, that he should attend the School of Fine Art in Madrid, qualify as a teacher and use his free time to paint as he liked. Dalí agreed with enthusiasm. He had been working hard and won two prizes. He was seventeen years of age and supremely confident of his ability. Suddenly Figueras was stifling, and Madrid offered independence, an escape from the watchful eyes of his family. Admission to the School of Fine Arts was dependent on an examination, a drawing of a classical

Accommodations of Desire, 1929
Les accommodations du désir
Oil on panel, 22 x 35 cm
Mr and Mrs Julien Levy Collection, New York

Desire for Dalí 'is expressed through the 'terrorizing images of lions' heads'.

17

The Enigma of Desire, 1929
L'énigme du désir
Oil on canvas, 110 x 150.7 cm
Bayerische Staatsgemälde-
sammlung, Staatsgalerie moderner
Kunst, Munich

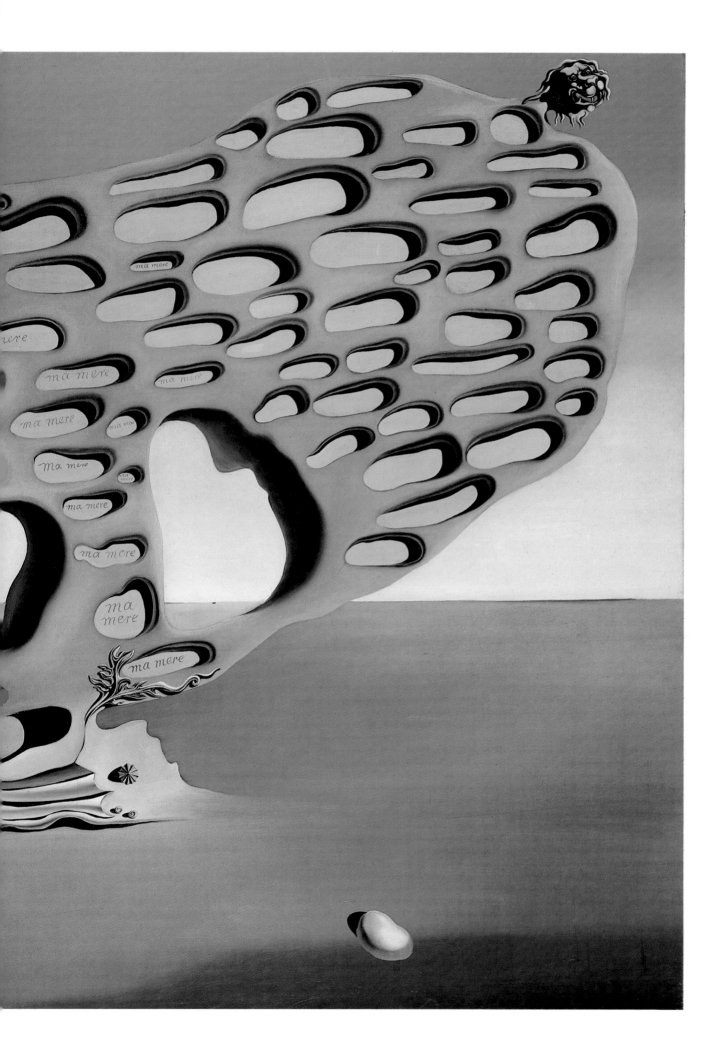

subject made to a specified size. According to Dalí's account, he chose to ignore the instructions completely, making the drawing too small. Redrawing, he made it too large. On the final day of submission, panic-stricken, he made another attempt, this time even smaller than the first. Nevertheless, so perfect was the study that he was accepted as a student.

For months he behaved as a model pupil. All social life was shunned. Sundays were spent at the Prado making Cubist sketches of the various paintings. He had just discovered one of the Cubist masters, Juan Gris, and was in full revolt against Impressionism. The rainbow palette was replaced with black, white, sienna and olive green. If the colours were sombre, the same could not be said of his attire. Long trousers were discarded in favour of short trousers with socks, sometimes puttees, a long waterproof cape, hair sticking out like a mane beneath a large black felt hat, and an unlit pipe clenched between his teeth. Whatever enthusiasm he had for the teaching ability at the Academy in the early months soon gave way to disappointment. He felt they had nothing to offer. To his searching questions about art, they had only evasive answers, such as: 'It's temperament that counts – no rules, no constraints. Simplify.' ' I was expecting to find limits, rigour, scholarship,' he remarked, 'I was offered liberty, laziness, approximations.' Yet he continued to be an exemplary student, never missing a class and always respectful. The professors found him cold, too cerebral, but clever and always successful with his work.

His growing frustration with the Academy is amusingly highlighted by the incident of the plaster. One day, entering the sculpture room during the lunch period, he emptied sacks of plaster into a basin under the

Scene from the film
L'Age d'Or, 1930
The Golden Age

After *Un Chien Andalou* in 1929, Dalí and Buñuel collaborated on a second Surrealist film financed by the Vicomte de Noailles in 1930. Dalí's scenario called for archbishops with embroidered tiaras bathing among the rocks of Cape Creus. He also suggested a few 'blasphemous scenes' which were to be presented with fanaticism in order to 'achieve the grandeur of a true and authentic sacrilege'.

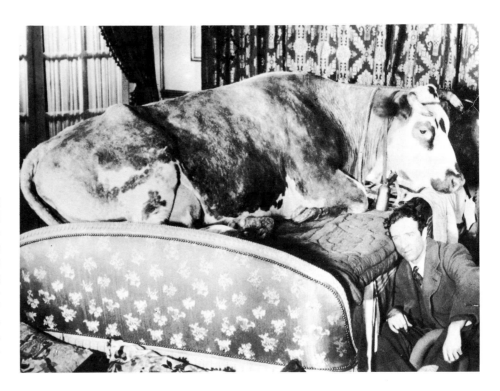

Page 23:
Nostalgia of the Cannibal, 1932
La nostalgie du cannibale
Oil on canvas, 47.2 x 47.4 cm
Sprengel Collection, Kunstmuseum,
Hanover

Page 22:
**The True Picture of Arnold Böcklin's
"Island of the Dead"
at the Hour of Angelus, 1932**
*Le vrai tableau de "L'île des morts"
d'Arnold Böcklin à l'heure de
l'Angélus*
Oil on canvas, 77.5 x 64.5 cm
Von-der-Heydt Museum, Wuppertal

The Fountain, 1930
La fontaine
Oil on panel, 66 x 41 cm
Collection of
Mr and Mrs A. Reynolds Morse,
Salvador Dalí Museum,
St. Petersburg (Florida)

running tap. Soon the floor was inundated with the milkwhite liquid which spread under the door and cascaded down the stairway to spill out into the entrance hall. Thoroughly alarmed by the magnitude of his action, he ploughed though the avalanche to the exit, but not before stopping to admire the fast-hardening mass.

It was about this time that he discovered Freud. *The Interpretation of Dreams* was of major importance in his life. The most casual act was subjected to agonizing self-analysis, and he was to go through tortures

Giorgio de Chirico
The Philosopher's Conquest, 1914
Oil on canvas, 125.7 x 100.3 cm
Joseph Winterbotham Collection,
Art Institute of Chicago

Dalí often made use of de Chirico's
deep perspective and the mystery of
his shadows.

trying to decide whether he was really mad. His dreams, he found, were always linked to an actual event, ending in the exact spot and the same situation in which he found himself upon awakening.

The artistic and literary developments in Europe, particularly Dadaism, with its mockery of all accepted values and sensational outbursts of exhibitionism, had not passed unnoticed among some of the students at the Academy. Luis Buñuel, Federico García Lorca, Pedro Garfias and Eugenio Montes were the moving spirits of this small but wild band in which Dalí was soon to occupy a position of importance. They praised his Cubist paintings, listened excitedly to his extravagant ideas. It was not long, he assures us, before it was 'Dalí this, Dalí that and Dalí everything'. It was all very exciting. He became an habitué of the cafes, joining in the noisy intellectual discussions on art and literature, women and sex. The outlandish clothes were discarded for expensive suits and silk shirts, the pallid face was streaked with make-up, and he took to plastering his hair down with picture varnish.

An act of rebellion in support of one of the teachers brought about his temporary suspension from the Academy for a year. He returned to his worried father in Figueras, where shortly afterwards he was arrested by the Guardia Civil and spent a month in prison. It was a period of considerable revolutionary agitation, and Dalí, with his wild talk of anarchy and monarchy, was immediately suspect. Since no charges could be found on which to try him, he was finally set free.

Again he left for Cadaqués, where he became an 'ascetic once more and where I literally gave myself over body and soul to painting and to my philosophic research'. He knew that once he returned to Madrid he would soon revert to the old ways. But in the meantime it was to be all discipline and work. 'I was in fact a monster,' he said, 'whose anatomical parts were an eye, a hand and a brain.'

At the end of the disciplinary period he returned to the Academy and immediately established his reputation for irreverence and rebellion. Given as a painting subject a Gothic statue of the Virgin, he chose to paint a pair of scales. 'Perhaps you see a virgin like everyone else,' he told the astonished teacher, 'I see a pair of scales.' There is little doubt that at this time Dalí was going through several opposing experiments in painting. He explored the problems of Italian Futurism, particularly their attempts to suggest objects in motion. From 1924 the interest shifted to the Scuola Metafisica (the Metaphysical School), a movement evolved by Giorgio de Chirico and Carlo Carrà.

De Chirico had had his art training in Munich, where he had come under the influence of the German Swiss, Arnold Böcklin, with all his mysticism and romanticism. Nietzsche's writing on *Symbolical Dream Pictures* and Schopenhauer's *Essay on Apparitions* were to contribute to his enigmatic and disquieting dream imagery. The mystery of his city streets and deserted squares, with their own laws of perspective and

veiled childhood memories, are some of the most poetic statements of our age. They proposed a rejection of Cubism and Futurism, affirming in their place an art of the metaphysical, a return to dreams and inner perception. In Paris the Surrealists had not failed to recognize the extreme originality of what de Chirico had achieved.

For Dalí, it was to bring him that step nearer the means of externalizing his obsessions. It was all the more surprising, therefore, in view of his later development in Surrealism and his vehement rejection of abstraction, that he should suddenly turn back to the Cubism of Picasso. James Thrall Soby puts forward the theory that 'Dalí had inevitably to face the issue which Cubism had raised in European art. Not to put too fine a point on it, this issue consisted in whether a given younger artist should be for or against Picasso's dictates', and he goes on to say: 'Remembering that Picasso was a fellow Catalan, one can understand why Dalí should have been caught, at some point, by the immense suction of his ideas.' Yet it is not inconceivable that Dalí sensed in the classical structure and abstracted subject-matter of Cubism a security that, at least for a time, would provide some steadying control over the disordered nature of his innermost thoughts, which were now beginning to possess him, thoughts that were no longer to lead a subjectively delusional existence only, but

The Persistence of Memory, 1931
La persistance de la mémoire
Oil on canvas, 24 x 33 cm
Museum of Modern Art, New York

Dalí said that eating Camembert cheese had inspired the limp watches: 'Be persuaded that Salvador Dalí's famous limp watches are nothing but the tender, extravagant and solitary paranoiac-critical Camembert of time and space.' This image was to make its appearance in many subsequent works.

Six Apparitions of Lenin on a Piano, 1931
Hallucination partielle. Six apparitions de Lénine sur un piano
Oil on canvas, 114 x 146 cm
Centre Pompidou, Musée National
d'Art Moderne, Paris

Although Dalí refused to associate himself with the revolutionary aspects of Surrealism, this painting was inspired by the leader of the Russian revolution. A less charitable portrayal of Lenin is to be seen in the painting *The Enigma of William Tell* (p. 37), painted in 1934.

Page 28:
Fried Eggs without the Plate, 1932
Oeufs sur le plat sans le plat
Oil on canvas, 60.4 x 42 cm
Collection of
Mr and Mrs A. Reynolds Morse,
Salvador Dalí Museum,
St. Petersburg (Florida)

The pun in the original French title is untranslatable into English.

Page 29:
Ordinary French Loaf with Two Fried Eggs Riding without a Plate, Trying to Sodomise a Crumb of Portuguese Bread, 1932
Pain français moyen avec deux oeufs sur le plat sans le plat,
à cheval, essayant de sodomiser une mie de pain portugais
Oil on wood, 16.8 x 32 cm
Takahashi Shoji Collection, Tokyo

The image of fried eggs was an 'ever-hallucinatory image' for Dalí, which he claimed to be able to produce at will by putting pressure on his closed eyes. Eggs appeared in a number of works around this period, including *Fried Eggs without the Plate* (p. 28).

were to be made objectively perceptible in painting. It is no accident that, after his rejection of Cubism, he should have painted *The Lugubrious Game* (p. 14), with its provocative scatology and in particular its coprophagic element.

Committing himself to Cubism, Dalí undertook a visit to Paris in 1927 to see Picasso. According to Dalí's account, he arrived deeply moved and full of respect. 'I have come to see you before visiting the Louvre,' he told the artist. 'You were quite right to do so,' replied Picasso. Dalí then showed him a small painting he had brought, which Picasso studied without comment. For the next two hours he contemplated the canvases that Picasso dragged from the studio, also without any comment. On his leaving, they exchanged glances which meant, Dalí assures us, 'You get the idea?' 'I get it.' Another account of this visit speaks of Dalí taking a tape measure with him and in complete silence proceeding to measure the size of each canvas placed before him.

After Dalí's return to Figueras, Luis Buñuel proposed collaboration on a film which his mother was prepared to finance. Dalí found the script naive and mediocre, and suggested in its place a scenario he had just completed. Its theme was 'adolescence and death'. Together they worked on the plot, and also the title – it was to be called *Un Chien Andalou*. Buñuel hurried back to Paris to undertake the production, while Dalí stayed behind to 'sharpen all my doctrinal tools at a distance'.

His solo exhibition at the Dalmau Gallery in Barcelona had been seen by Picasso during a brief visit to that city. Back in Paris he had spoken enthusiastically about the show to his dealer, Paul Rosenberg, who wrote asking for photographs, which Dalí neglected to send. 'I knew,' he said, 'that the day I arrived in Paris, I would merely have got them back.' Another Spanish painter, Joan Miró, wrote and followed this up with a visit to Figueras with his gallery director, Pierre Loeb. For all Miró's generous support, Loeb remained sceptical, finding Dalí's painting too confusing and lacking in personality. Dalí must have found it a disappointment. Paris was where the battle was being fought and he intended, somehow, to participate in it. His exhibitions in Barcelona and Madrid had been highly successful, the reviews flattering. The magazine *d'Aci, d'Alla* had written: 'We are absolutely certain that if the young artist does not leave us, he will be one of those who will give the greatest glory to Catalan painting in our century . . .' *La Publicidad* could not find among the young painters a more fascinating figure than that of this young man from Figueras. With the attention Dalí was also getting from Paris, the very centre of the art world, his father was finally convinced that he should go. It was 1928 when Dalí arrived in Paris. He was not thinking of another visit to Picasso, but, as he tells us, he turned to the taxi driver and asked, 'Do you know any good whorehouses?' 'Get in, Monsieur,' he answered, with somewhat wounded pride, though in a fatherly way. 'Don't worry, I know them all.'

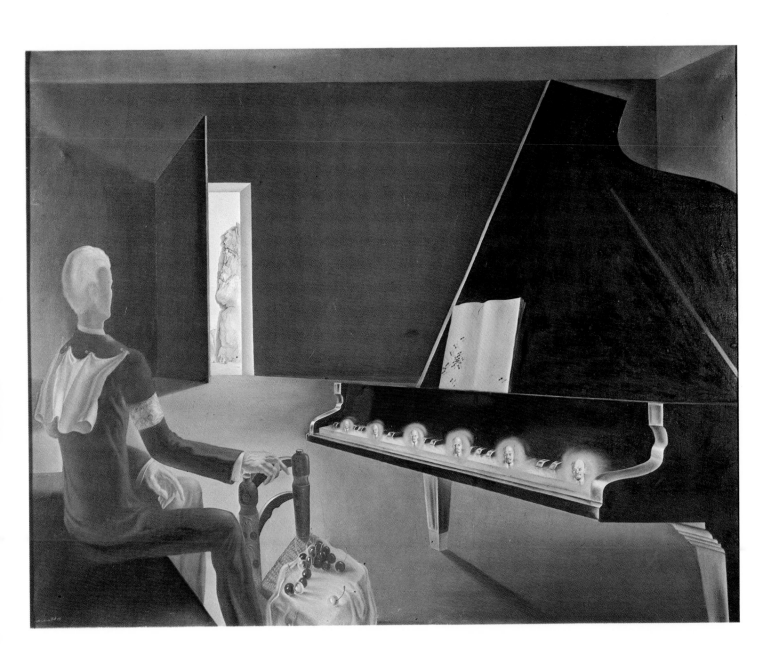

The Birth of Liquid Desires, 1932
La naissance des désirs liquides
Oil on canvas, 95 x 112 cm
Peggy Guggenheim Collection,
Venice

"When I paint, the sea roars. The others splash about in the bath."
Salvador Dalí

He visited the 'Chabanais' which must have impressed him, for some twelve years later, speaking of the three spots that produced in him the deepest sense of mystery, he cited the stairway of the 'Chabanais' for its ugly eroticism, Palladio's Theatre in Vicenza for its divine aesthetic, and the entrance to the tombs of the Spanish kings at El Escorial as the 'most mysterious and beautiful mortuary spot'.

Miró did not desert his young friend and was full of advice on how to go about making the right connections in Paris society. First, he must get a dinner jacket. He must not talk too much and must keep fit. Tomorrow he would meet Tristan Tzara, the Dadaist leader. The social rounds continued – the Duchesse de Dato, the Comtesse Cuevas de Vera, Goemans, who was to become his dealer, Pavlik Tchletichev, Robert Desnos, who wanted to buy his painting *The First Days of Spring* (p. 15). Pierre Loeb, who still hoped one day to do a Dalí exhibition, took him to the Bal Tabarin, where he met that 'legendary being,' Paul Eluard, the Surrealist poet. He looked in on Buñuel. *Un Chien Andalou* was going into production, and he helped with some of the effects. The requirements were formidable – a nude model who was to have live sea-urchins under each arm, several decomposed donkeys, a grand piano, a severed hand, three ants' nests and a cow's eye.

The winter of 1929 saw the first showing of *Un Chien Andalou*. Praised by the Surrealists for its dream sequences and arresting imagery, the audience had little stomach for a film that opened with a woman's eye being sliced by a razor in close-up.

The following year saw their second film *L'Age d'Or (The Golden Age)* (p. 20), financed by the Vicomte de Noailles. Full of violence and revolt, it showed archbishops and bones among the rocks of Cape Creus, a blind man being ill-treated, a dog crushed to death, a son killed by his father, and a character from de Sade disguised as Christ. Violence broke out, with the right-wing pro-Hitler group, the 'Camelots du roy', and the cinema was wrecked. The police intervened and further showings were banned.

For all Dalí's frenetic activity, the success which he so desperately sought did not come. It was an intolerable situation. Shunning his new-found friends to spend hours sitting in cafés or wandering the boulevards, he felt again the touch of madness. The following evening 'I thus hung my illness on the coat-hanger of the Gare d'Orsay . . .' He caught a train for Spain.

Back in Cadaqués the recent events disappeared, replaced with the wonders and fantasies of childhood. Strange images, he tells us, took possession of his mind, rising enigmatically from the dark. The immediate thought was to make a painting to reproduce each image in all its clarity and as scrupulously as possible. It would be completely automatic, without conscious intervention, obeying only his authentic, biological desire. *The Lugubrious Game* (p. 14) – the title was suggested by Eluard – was

Dalí's first truly Surrealist painting. In his autobiography he subsequently wrote: 'This work, unusual and disconcerting in the highest degree, was by the very physiology of its elaboration far removed from the "Dadaist collae", which is always a poetic and *a posteriori* arrangement. It was also the contrary of Chirico's metaphysical painting, for here the spectator had perforce to believe in the earthy reality of the subject, which was one of an elementary and frenzied biological nature. And it was furthermore the contrary of the poetic softening of certain abstract paintings which continue stupidly, like blind moths, to bump into the extinguished lamps of the neo-Platonic light.

'I, then, and only I was the true Surrealist painter, at least according to the definition which its chief, André Breton, gave of Surrealism. Nevertheless, when Breton saw this painting, he hesitated for a long time before its scatological elements, for in the picture appeared a figure seen from behind, whose drawers were bespattered with excrement. The involuntary aspect of this element, so characteristic in psychopathological

Memory of the Child-Woman, 1932
La mémoire de la femme-enfant
Oil on canvas, 99 x 119.5 cm
Collection of
Mr and Mrs A. Reynolds Morse,
Salvador Dalí Museum,
St. Petersburg, Florida

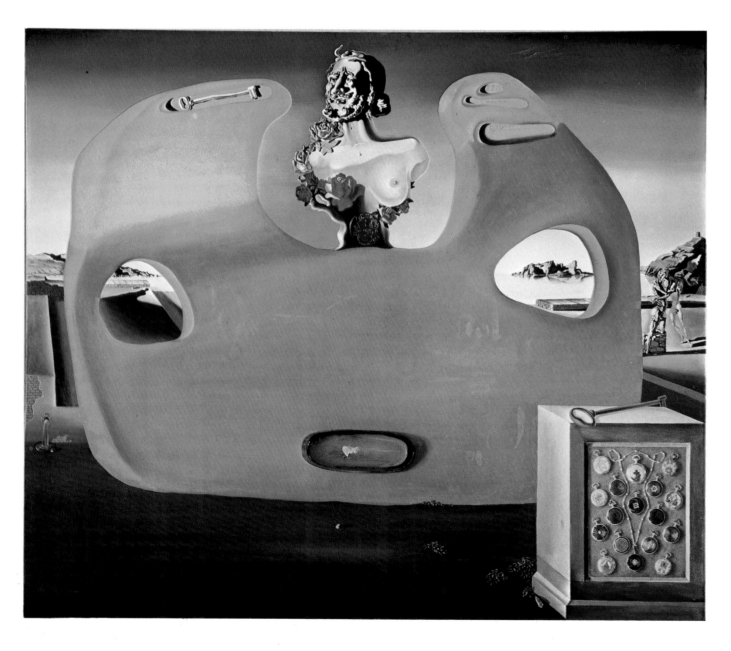

iconography, should have sufficed to enlighten him. But I was obliged to justify myself by saying that it was merely a simulacrum. No further questions were asked. But had I been pressed, I should certainly have had to answer that it was the simulacrum of the excrement itself. This idealistic narrowness was, from my point of view, the fundamental "intellectual vice" of the early period of Surrealism. Hierarchies were established where there was no need for any. Between the excrement and a piece of

Atavistic Ruins after the Rain, 1934
Vestiges ataviques après la pluie
Oil on canvas, 65 x 54 cm
Perls Galleries, New York

Average Atmospherocephalic Bureaucrat in the Act of Milking a Cranial Harp, 1933
Bureaucrate moyen atmosphérocéphale dans l'attitude de traire du lait d'une harpe crânienne
Oil on canvas, 22 x 16.5 cm
Collection of
Mr and Mrs A. Reynolds Morse,
Salvador Dalí Museum,
St. Petersburg, Florida

rock crystal, by the very fact that they both sprang from the common basis of the unconscious, there could and should be no categorical difference. And these were the men who denied the hierarchies of tradition!'

During this period in Cadaqués, there was to be a deepening of his visionary imagination, an inextinguishable fecundity of experiments and an enrichment of his technique. His sympathies were now wholeheartedly with the Surrealists. The summer of 1929 saw not only *The Lugubrious Game* (p.14) but also *Accommodations of Desire* (p. 17) in which he turned to collage, the pasting of photographic or engraved elements on to his canvas. He used this not as Picasso and the Cubists had done, as a formal means and an extension of the painter's palette, integrating the painted cuttings with the brushwork in a purely textural way. Instead he exploited

Skull with its Lyrical Appendage Leaning on a Night Table Which Ought to Be the Temperature of a Cardinal's Nest, 1934
Crâne avec son appendice lyrique reposant sur une table de nuit qui devrait avoir la même température que le nid d'un cardinal
Oil on panel, 24 x 19 cm
Collection of
Mr and Mrs A. Reynolds Morse,
Salvador Dalí Museum,
St. Petersburg, Florida

the disruptive potential of collage. Rather than playing down the subject-matter, he used it to dramatize the psychological and social objectives, with the pictorial aspect always used as a vehicle for the communication of ideas. Although the head of the lion is a photographic cut-out, the overall exactitude of the other areas in the work is so perfect that we are confused by what is collage and what is paint.

Of the same year is *Illumined Pleasures* (p. 16), which clearly reveals his growing debt to de Chirico in the framed paintings within the painting and the unreal use of colour to suggest a dreamlike atmosphere. It is particularly noticeable for its photographic realism which gives such credibility to the most irrational subject matter. In his insistence on obeying the dictates of the unconscious, Dalí set up his easel at the foot of the bed so that before going to sleep he could fix his mind on the unfinished painting to link his sleep with its further development. At other times he would 'wait whole hours without any such images occurring. Then, not painting, I would remain in suspense . . .' or would try by all possible means to simulate madness. Visions of 'three tiny curates running very fast in single file across a little Japanese gangplank . . .'

The Phantom Cart, 1933
La charrette fantôme
Oil on panel, 19 x 24.1 cm
Private collection

One of Dalí's more lyrical works which preceded the 'Beach at Rosas' series of 1934-36. The two figures seated in the cart are also the buildings of the distant towns, suggesting that the cart has already reached its destination.

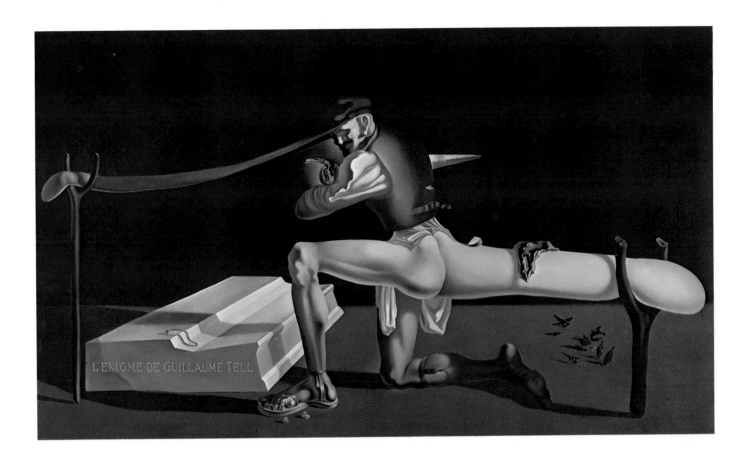

L'ENIGME DE GUILLAUME TELL

would set him off into fits of laughter. Again, he imagined owls perched on peoples' heads, surmounted by pieces of excrement. Free from all reason, he recorded it all with maniacal care.

In the meantime, Camille Goemans arranged to put on his first Paris exhibition late in 1929. Dalí was to receive 3,000 francs for all the works he produced during the summer. Goemans would take a percentage on the sales and have three canvases of his choice. It was an instant success with almost all the paintings sold at between six and twelve thousand francs. *The Lugubrious Game* was bought by the Vicomte de Noailles, who later was to acquire so many of his works.

It was not long before the Surrealists recognized the significant contribution that Dalí could now make to the movement. His belief in the superiority of association, the omnipotence of dreams and the element of chance were seen as means to an end and an instrument of exploration and discovery. His statement that he was completely uninterested in all aesthetic values and painterly qualities, concerned only with depicting the images of the irrational, was in line with Surrealism's avowed claim that the use of a technique was but a means to an end, that of reconciling man and the universe. During the following weeks Buñuel, Magritte and his wife Georgette, and Paul Eluard and his wife Gala arrived in Cadaqués. They were distressed by his continuing fits of convulsive laughter and general mental state, and also concerned about his painting *The Lugubrious Game* (p. 14). Eluard suggested Gala approach him on the subject. Did the picture, with its realistic spattering of excrement on the man's

The Enigma of William Tell, 1933
L'énigme de Guillaume Tell
Oil on canvas, 201.4 x 346 cm
Moderna Museet, Stockholm

The legend of William Tell was reinterpreted by Dalí as one of incestuous mutilation. Although devoted to his father, Dalí rebelled against his authority, a situation which eventually led to his being thrown out of his father's home. The fond relationship between father and son in the legend was to become a thematic obsession for a number of important works: *William Tell*, painted in 1930, and *The Old Age of William Tell* of 1931. This particular painting, in which Lenin appears trouserless and with an extended buttock, combined with Dalí's reactionary political tendencies, was to bring about his first break with Surrealists.

Some years later Dalí made the following comment about the painting: 'William Tell, a fatherly phantasm, has placed a mutton chop on my head, indicating the desire to eat the infant Dalí, whom he carries in his arms.'

Portrait of Freud, 1938
Portrait de Freud
Indian ink on paper, 29.5 x 26.5 cm
Edward James Foundation, West
Dean

**The Ghost of Vermeer of Delft Which
Can Be Used as a Table, 1934**
*Le spectre de Vermeer van Delft pouv-
ant être utilisé comme table*
*(théorie phénoménologique du "meu-
ble-aliment")*
Oil on panel, 18 x 14 cm
Collection of Mr and Mrs A. Reynolds Morse,
Salvador Dalí Museum, St. Petersburg, Florida

Dalí's obsession with food and furniture probably prompted this painting,
as well as his respect for the art of
Vermeer. He said of this work, 'A
spectre that could be used as a table:
an eminently eucharistic idea for a
painting.'

rear, refer in any way to his life? Was he in fact a coprophagic? In any case it was felt that the work was weakened by its propagandist character as a psychopathological document.

Dalí assured her that he had no liking for that type of aberration, but did 'consider scatology as a terrifying element, just as I do blood, or my phobia for grasshoppers'.

This period saw the beginning of his great love for Gala. In his usual way he went to inordinate lengths to attract her. Taking his best shirt he cut it short enough to expose his navel, then tore it on the shoulder and the chest. The collar was entirely removed. He turned his trousers inside out. He shaved his armpits and then dyed then with laundry blue. Not completely satisfied, he removed the blue and shaved until his armpits were bloody, then did the same to his knees. For perfume he could find only Eau de Cologne, which made him sick; so he boiled fish glue and water, adding some goat manure and a touch of aspic, making a paste which he rubbed all over his body. He was ready to meet her. Then he saw her through the window and realized that the whole get-up was a nuptial costume. Hurriedly changing, washing off the stench of the concoction as well as possible, he ran to meet her only to collapse at her feet in hysterical laughter.

Gala's initial reaction was not favourable. She thought him obnoxious and unbearable, yet intuition told her that his hysteria was not gaiety nor scepticism, but fanaticism. They began to rely increasingly on each other. One day, when he threw himself at her feet, she cried out: 'My little boy! We shall never leave each other.'

Gala was a formidable woman. Elena Dimitrovna Diakonova was born in Russia and began a career as a full-time muse in 1917 when she married Paul Eluard. A siren for many of the Surrealists, she tempted Max Ernst away from his wife and child, and he joined the Eluards for a *ménage à trois* in their villa at Eaubonne. After transferring her affections and ellegiance to Dalí, she became his business manager, inspiration and virago muse. Sterile following an operation to remove a uterine tumour in 1931, she was perhaps the perfect sex object for Dalí, who was always happiest keeping women at a voyeuristic distance.

Dalí was now working on a portrait of Paul Eluard and two other large canvases. One was to create a scandal. It represented, he tells us, 'a large head, livid as wax, the cheeks very pink, the eyelashes long, and the impressive nose pressed against the earth. This face has no mouth, and in its place was stuck an enormous grasshopper. The grasshopper's belly was decomposed, and full of ants. Several of these ants scurried across the space that should have been filled by the mouth of the great anguished face, whose head terminated in architecture and ornamentations of the style of 1900.' He called the painting *The Great Masturbator* (1929).

His works all packed for his forthcoming exhibition, he again set off for Paris. This time he was planning to join the Surrealist group.

It is perhaps necessary to pause for a moment while we consider the
development of Surrealist painting and the position it had arrived at
around the time of Dalí's intervention. While it would be impossible to
summarize here all the various manifestations that determined the principles on which it rests and continues to build, we can consider some of its
fundamental aims.

The first foundations of Surrealism were laid in 1924, the year of the
first Surrealist manifesto by André Breton. Surrealism dedicated itself to
a far more systematic revision of values and an approach towards the
subconscious as the essential source of all art, following the disruptive and
anarchistic action of Dada, which had died in 1922. As a result, a definition was made, dictionary style: 'SURREALISM, n, Pure psychic automatism, by which it is intended to express, verbally, in writing, or by other
means, the real process of thought. Thought's dictation, in the absence of
all control exercised by reason and outside all aesthetic or moral preoccupations. ENCYCL. philos. Surrealism rests on the belief in the superior
reality of forms of association neglected heretofore, in the omnipotence
of the dream and in the disinterested play of thought. It tends definitely to
destroy all other psychic mechanisms and to substitute itself in the solu-
tion of the principal problems of life.'[2]

The essential spirit of Surrealism, at that time, was clearly formulated.
It was a purely intuitive period. 'I believe,' said Breton, 'in the future
resolution of the states of dream and reality, in appearances that are
accordingly contradictory, in a sort of absolute reality, or *surréalité*, if I
may so call it.'

No conception of Surrealist painting existed then. In fact it was difficult
to see how it could transcend 'all aesthetic . . . preoccupations'. Only in
automatic writing, in fantasies and states of hallucination could the
stream of the unconscious emerge. Indeed, Pierre Naville, in 1925, expressed the view that there could be no such thing as Surrealist Painting.
The whole idea was a contradiction in terms. Breton did not see the
definition as quite so rigid. In the same year he published an article, under
the still hesitant title *Surrealism and Painting*, in which he declared that
'Painting could supply the rhythmic unity', and there could be an art as 'an
instrument of discovery'. Surrealist identity would hinge on the
methodological and iconographic relevance of the picture to the main
ideas of the movement – that is, to automatism and the 'dream image'.
The automatism of painters like Miró and André Masson was the equiva-
lent of the free verbal association which the writer practised. The artist
had merely to let his brush wander freely over the surface. 'Rather than
setting out to paint something,' Miró explained, 'I begin painting, and as I
paint the picture begins to assert itself, or suggest itself under my brush.
The form becomes the sign for a woman or a bird as I work . . . The first
stage is free, unconscious . . .'

In other words, Surrealism from the beginning excluded the rational

Mae West's Face Which Can Be Used as a Surrealist Apartment, 1934-35
Visage de Mae West, pouvant être utilisé comme appartement surréaliste
Gouache on newspaper, 31 x 17 cm
Art Institute of Chicago

The furnishings of a room are transformed into a portrait of Mae West. Edward James later had a real lip sofa made along the lines of the one in the painting.

Pages 44/45:
Anthropomorphic Chest-of-Drawers, 1936
Le cabinet anthropomorphique
Oil on wood, 25.4 x 44.2 cm
Kunstsammlung Nordrhein-Westfalen, Düsseldorf

and the logical in favour of the irrational. Painters were urged not to draw their inspiration from reality, but from a 'purely interior model' which was defined in those painters who genuinely rediscovered the reason for painting. 'These,' said Breton, 'were Picasso, Max Ernst, Masson, Miró, Tanguy, Arp, Picabia and Man Ray. It was not the artistic quality that was important, but its Surrealist quality. Only its hidden content was of value. This motivation reveals the difference between Surrealist painting and other forms of artistic creation under the sway of aesthetic considerations.'

While automatism still remains today the best-known method of tapping the resources of the unconscious, the Surrealists were not unaware of the inherent weaknesses in the process. Breton, speaking of the definition of Surrealism offered in 1924, admitted '... that I deceived myself at the time in advocating the use of an automatic thought not only removed from all control exercised by the reason, but also disengaged from "all conscious aesthetic or moral preoccupations". It should at least have said: "all aesthetic or moral preoccupations". 'Fascinating though the automatic approach might be, the imagination has a habit of repeating itself indefinitely. An element of monotony and repetition creeps into unconscious experience. By 1928 many of the Surrealist painters were in the process of working out a method by which the discoveries made by chance could be completed by the intervention of the artist himself, in order to achieve the full realization of what was inspired by the automatic process. In other words, some degree of control would be necessary.

Dalí shared the Surrealists' faith in adapting the automatic processes to painting, in recording the involuntary images inspired by dreams. He also saw that, for the imagery to achieve its full potentiality, it had to be developed in a fully conscious way. It did not mean that he arrested the process of free association by which one image suggested another, but that he sought to elaborate his psychic revelations with all the precision and artistic skill at his command, in a conscious and deliberate manner. 'Handmade photography' was the term he used to describe his technique, by which he meant that his painting would be indistinguishable from photography and therefore more believable. Even the size of many of these paintings was no larger than the average photograph.

The Freudian basis of Surrealism was clearly defined between the first manifesto of 1924 and the second manifesto of 1929. Technically, the paintings of that period fall roughly into two groups.

The first is the intuitive, spontaneous approach of Masson and Miró, with its allegiance to dreams, folly and the incoherent. Breton proposed the unbridled imagination, and if it contradicted that which was known, all the better.

The second type of Surrealist painting draws on a meticulously realistic technique by which the identity of the object is firmly designated. In this category is found the art of such painters as Magritte, Brauner and Dalí.

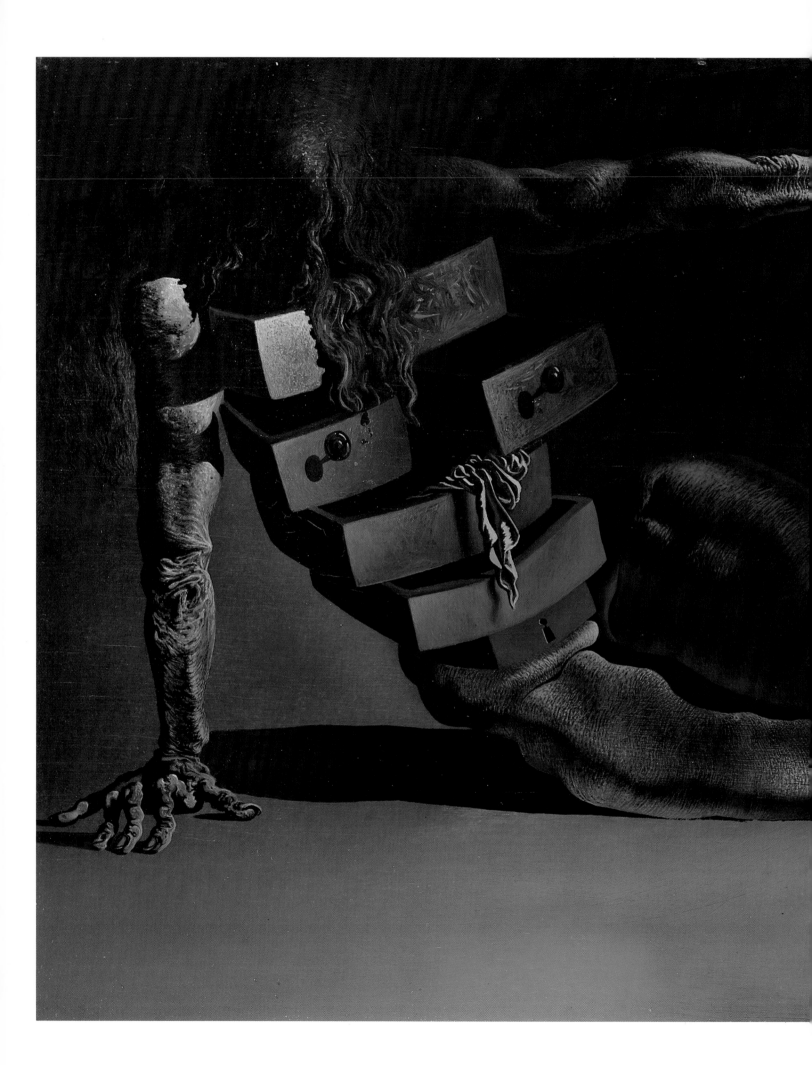

Yet there is one important difference in Dalí's use of his technical ability, namely that he put it at the service of automatism and passivity. At the same time he was to revive, with his convincingly illusionist realism, the theory of painting as an illustrative medium and to champion a return of the anecdote to art. It was a contribution of major importance to Surrealism at that time and gave a new impetus to experiments that were still at a tentative stage.

Breton may have been aware, even that early, of the risks that Dalí might face. In his introduction to the 1929 exhibition he wrote: 'Dalí is like a man who hesitates between talent and genius, or as one might once have said, between vice and virtue. He is one of those who arrive from so far away that one barely has time to see them enter – only enter. He takes his place, without saying a word, in a system of interference.' He continues in a later paragraph: 'On the other hand there is hope: hope that not everything will become so dark that even the admirable voice which is Dalí's will break when it reaches one's ears, even though certain "materialists" are anxious that the sound of it should be confused with the creaking of his patent leather shoes . . .'[3] Whatever doubts were felt, the importance accorded to him was clearly stated: 'With the coming of Dalí, it is perhaps the first time that the mental windows have been opened really wide, so that one can feel oneself gliding up towards the predatory sky's trapdoor.'[4]

The originality of Dalí, the revolutionary critical interpretation he brought to bear upon familiar works of art, his translation of hallucinations and dreams into a concrete reality, and his fascination with all forms of aberration were all essential to Surrealist aims at that time. His understanding of Freud, on which so much of his work was to be based, led to

Lobster Telephone, 1936
Téléphone-homard
Assemblage, 15 x 30 x 17 cm
Edward James Foundation,
Tate Gallery, London

Dalí made a number of Surrealist objects for his English patron, Edward James, including the famous 'Lobster-Telephone'. It illustrates his fascination with giving life to the inanimate.

the development of his theories of the 'paranoiac method'. In his book *The Visible Woman* he described it as 'a spontaneous method of irrational knowledge based upon the critical and systematic objectification of delirious associations and interpretations'. In simple terms it was a form of image interpretation, in which the spectator sees in a picture a different image depending on the imaginative ability of the onlooker. For instance, one might see, in a stain on the wall, a face, a castle or a galloping horse. A postcard of a group of negroes sitting around their hut had only to be seen from another angle to become a portrait of André Breton. (Breton insisted it was of the Marquis de Sade.) It was to become the subject for a future painting.

Not unrelated to the paranoiac method is Lautréamont's image, 'beautiful as the chance meeting upon a dissecting table of a sewing machine and an umbrella'. In Freudian terms we recognize the sewing machine as a woman, the umbrella as a man and the dissecting table as a bed. The sewing machine and the umbrella will make love.

Paranoiac-Critical Solitude, 1935
Solitude paranoïaque-critique
Oil on panel, 19 x 23 cm
Private collection

The treatment of the car in this painting is characteristic of his contempt for the mechanical and for industrialism. Here the vehicle has been excavated fossil-like from the rock.

Pages 48/49:
The Chemist of Ampurdan Looking for Absolutely Nothing, 1936
Le pharmacien d'Ampurdan ne cherchant absolument rien
Oil on wood, 30 x 52 cm
Folkwang Museum, Essen

47

Dalí envisaged the possibilities of giving objective value on the plane of reality to his world of irrational experiences. The paranoiac-critical activity became a system of revealing images and associations. Like other methods used by the Surrealists, it was a means of forcing inspiration.[5] The interpretative system of paranoiac-critical activity led Dalí to transform Jean-François Millet's *Angelus* into a painting of extreme eroticism. He found that the man on the left was using his hat to hide his turgescent sex, that the woman was pregnant, and that the pitchfork, thrust into the ground alongside the open sack of potatoes, symbolised the male sex and the sack of potatoes the female. Dalí maintained that the immense success of the picture, its devout subject-matter apart, was entirely due to its latent content.

He was to produce a number of pictures on this theme; for instance, *Gala and the 'Angelus' of Millet Immediately Preceding the Arrival of the Conic Anamorphoses*, illustrated in *Le Surréalisme au Service de la Revolution*, No. 6, 1933, and *Meditation upon the Harp*. Both executed

Medianimic-Paranoiac Image, 1935
Image médiumnique-paranoïaque
Oil on panel, 19 x 23 cm
Private collection

Another painting of the Rosas series in which the fixtures take on a phantom-like effect.

between 1932 and 1935, they are two examples in which be applied the method to the obsessional character of the *Angelus*.

Another artistic theme was launched when he discovered in the legend of William Tell not the filial devotion that people saw, but incestuous mutilation. It is explored in *William Tell* (1930), *The Enigma of William Tell* (p. 37) and *The Old Age of William Tell* (1931). Dalí's talent for parading his irrational delirium, his lurid taste for the sensational, was working overtime. He asserted his taste for chromolithographs (a picture printed in colours from stone) as 'the least accidental imitations of nature', and threw light on his own work which he described as 'instantaneous photography in colours and with images that are super-fine, extravagant, extra-plastic, extra-pictorial, unexplored, super-pictorial, superplastic, deceptive, hypernormal, feeble and of concrete irrationality'.

Morphological Echo, 1936
Echó morphologique
Oil on panel, 30.5 x 32.5 cm
Collection of
Mr and Mrs A. Reynolds Morse,
Salvador Dalí Museum,
St. Petersburg, Florida

51

Outskirts of Paranoiac-Critical Town, 1936
Banlieue de la ville paranoïaque-critique: après-midi sur la lisière de l'histoire européenne
Oil on panel, 46 x 66 cm
Private collection

The outline of the distant bell tower is duplicated in the foreground structure, through which is seen the skipping girl who also becomes the bell in the tower. Dalí made a painting of this detail in 1935, called *Nostalgic Echo*. The woman holding up a bunch of grapes is a portrait of Gala.

It is of course possible to accept the iconography of his work, as Dalí himself would insist, without asking what each detail might mean. Yet we know from his own account, not only of his childhood, but of the interpretative studies he has made of Millet, William Tell, the Pre-Raphaelites and others, that there is evidence of a specific meaning behind most of the imagery that finds it way into the paintings. Some, to which he attaches particular importance, are also unforgettable, like the crutches and limp watches. Others, more alarming, he tried to come to terms with by putting them down on canvas. Grasshoppers, for which he had a morbid fear, were identified with dislike for his father. Excrement was seen as 'the terrorising element'. Teeth are a Freudian sex symbol. Blood, forced into his eyes by hanging or swinging his head, provoked retinal illusions. Putrefaction had the hard light of gems. Death he saw as always being beautiful, just as eroticism must always be ugly. Implements, such as sharp instruments, are symbolic of mutilation. He considered that the three cardinal images of life were excrement, blood and putrefaction. 'We have long since learned to recognize the image of desire in images of terror', said David Gascoyne.[6]

Since his early childhood, Dalí was drawn to Vermeer of Delft. No painter has had such a devoted disciple, and Vermeer is probably the only painter he has ever made a copy of. According to Fleur Cowles,[7] the banker-collector Robert Lehman asked him to copy a Vermeer. Dalí assured him it was impossible, but in the early 1960s, some twenty years later, in a special room set aside in the Louvre, after exhaustive tests and analysis of colours and pigments, minute study of the way paint was applied down to the width of the brush required, Dalí went through a number of violent intellectual efforts to put himself in a state of receptivity. Suddenly he claimed to have discovered something extraordinary in the painting, which should not have been there. Immediately the experts gathered around with their magnifying glasses, until one discovered the hair from a paint brush hidden between the brush strokes, and the source of Dalí's discomfort was revealed. Relieved, he then sat before his canvas and proceeded to draw a rhinoceros horn, in the structure of which he saw the origin of all life. The image recurred in a number of works, including *The Maximum Speed of Raphael's Madonna* (1951); its perfect logarithmic spiral has Platonic implications for Dalí.

The influence of Vermeer on his own work is to be seen in a number of paintings: *The Image Disappears* (1934), and more directly in *The Ghost of Vermeer of Delft which can be used as a Table* (p. 39). Food was always one of Dalí's obsessions.[8] It occurs repeatedly in his autobiography: the prologue opens with, 'At the age of six I wanted to be a cook.' Such words as 'spinach', 'shellfish', 'cannibalism', 'bones' and 'caviar' are frequently used to describe paintings. It led him to paint a portrait of Gala with two

Three Young Women with Heads of Flowers Finding the Skin of a Grand Piano on the Beach, 1936
Femmes aux têtes de fleurs retrouvant sur la plage la dépouille d'un piano à queue
Oil on canvas, 54 x 65 cm
Collection of
Mr and Mrs A. Reynolds Morse,
Salvador Dalí Museum,
St. Petersburg, Florida

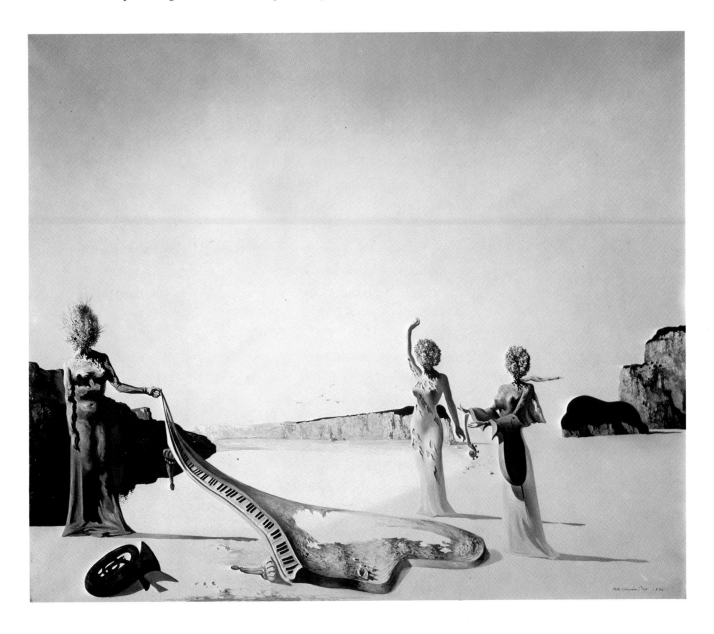

Autumn Cannibalism, 1936-37
Cannibalisme de l'automne
Oil on canvas, 65 x 65.2 cm
Edward James Foundation,
Tate Gallery, London

One of Dalí's most remarkable works
and an astonishing triumph of imagination. Food was always one of Dalí's
obsessions: 'Cooking is very close to
painting,' he once said. 'When you
are making a dish you add a little of
this and a little of that … it's like
mixing paints.' In this painting of two
beings in the act of devouring each
other a number of familiar Dalían images appear – crutches, bread, ants as
well as the instruments of mutilation.

lamb chops on her shoulder, as well as *The Weaning of Furniture-Nutri-
tion*. Cooking turkey without killing it was one of his culinary refine-
ments, and once he conceived the idea of making a table of egg-white so
that it could be eaten. 'Cooking is very close to painting,' he insisted. His
devotion to food and Vermeer might explain why *The Ghost of Vermeer*
(p. 39) suggests that it could be used as a dining table. If Vermeer has top
marks in his gallery of painters, Velázquez runs him a close second, failing
only in inspiration and mystery.[9] Applying his paranoiac-critical facility,
he saw the apparition of Velázquez's Infanta in the top of a Hindu temple.
More significantly, it is Velázquez's technical brilliance and richness of
colour that are the lyrical inspiration for *Apparition of Face and Fruit-
Dish on a Beach* (p. 65). This painting is also an exploration into the use of
the multiple image. The base of the fruit-dish is a rear view of his
childhood nurse, and forms the nose and mouth of the face, while the fruit
and the coastline are metamorphosed into a dog.

History provides many such examples of the fantastic in art: distorted
perspective, composite images, Bosch's highly personal visions, and the
use of the double image by the late 16th-century painter Arcimboldo.
They were all put to use by the Surrealists, who had first rejected the
rational basis on which these techniques were founded. They demonstrated that every form of the strange and mad could work in the cause of
art and take it beyond its own limits. Dalí's acceptance of every form of
madness took him further than the other Surrealists. By simulating the
disordered mind of the paranoiac, he became hypersensitive to hidden
appearances and counter-appearances, seeing not two or three images
but a sequence of images limited only by the mind's capacity. In *The
Endless Enigma* (1938) six concealed images are represented in the
painting. Less complex is *Old Age, Adolescence, Infancy* (1940). Dalí
maintained that the delirious image suggested by an initial object might
be the true reality. In *The Visible Women* he wrote: 'I challenge materialists to enquire into the more complex problem as to which of these images
has the highest probability of existence if the intervention of desire is
taken into account.' The 'omnipotence of desire,' said Breton, 'has
remained, since the beginning, Surrealism's sole act of faith'. The inten-
sity of Dalí's hallucinatory powers makes others believe in the reality of
what he sees. In truth he could say that the putrefaction of a donkey can
be considered as 'the hard and blinding flash of new gems'.

One of his more subtle uses of the double image is to be seen in the
painting entitled *Spain* (p. 67). The group of horsemen and figures in
combat, forming the face of the woman, owes an unmistakeable debt to
Leonardo, another painter of the past whom he now admired. They both
shared a common foundation of inventiveness. And Dalí was undoub-
tedly familiar with Freud's study of Leonardo, as well as that artist's
advice to look at the damp stains on walls in which one might see all kinds
of strange and imaginary images.

'The abject misery of abstract creation'[10] is the chapter heading to Dalí's attack on abstract art. He saw in it a lack of philosophical and general culture and evidence of mental debility, offering us 'upon the fresh optimism of their shiny paper the soup of the abstract aesthetic, which really and truly is even worse than the cold and revolting sordid vermicelli soups of neo-Thomism, which even the most convulsively hungry cats would not go near'.

As an antidote to its influence and to that of Negro art, which Picasso and other painters were extolling in Paris, Dalí upheld the decoration and architecture of Art Nouveau, which he considered as 'the psychopathological end-product of the Greco-Roman decadence', finding in the

Metamorphosis of Narcissus, 1937
Métamorphose de Narcisse
Oil on canvas, 50.8 x 78.3 cm
Edward James Foundation,
Tate Gallery, London

Dalí explained this painting to Freud when they met in London in 1938, prompting Freud to remark: 'I have never seen a more perfect specimen of a Spaniard. What a fanatic!' The work was provided with a literary commentary in a poem Dalí wrote at the same time, on the theme of death and fossilization of Narcissus.

ornamentation of the entrances to the Paris Metro a wrought-iron vegetation full of mystery, eroticism and perversity.

The imaginative dream structures of Antoni Gaudí in Barcelona, houses 'created for madmen, for erotomaniacs', were very familiar to Dalí. Güell Park, and the Basilica of the Church of the Holy Family, suggested 'in the most material way the persistence of dreams in the face of reality'.

Many of the 'undulant-convulsive' forms in his paintings between 1930 and 1934 are traceable to the ornamental elements of Art Nouveau around 1900. In the faces of these hysterical sculptures he saw the madwomen, treated by Dr Charcot at the mental hospital of Salpêtrière.

Pages 58/59:
Sleep, 1937
Le sommeil
Oil on canvas, 50 x 77 cm
Private Collection

Dalí saw sleep as a monster supported by crutches.

In *The Fountain* (p.21), with its shapes like wavy petrified hair, a certain sense of delirium interacts with the more convoluted excesses of the Art Nouveau style. The painting shows, too, his growing interest in the emotive value of the deep perspective that he saw in certain canvases of de Chirico. But whereas de Chirico was motivated by the mystery hiding behind normal relationships, Dalí evokes a delirious world of clinical irrationality bathed in an iridescent light. What he does share with de Chirico is the ability to project his apparent dislocations with the same acceptability, in spite of the inordinate nature of the imagery. *The Invisible Man,* which he started in 1929, did not escape the influence of Art Nouveau, recognizable in the treatment of the 'vaginal head' of the figure, as well as the sensuous ornamentation of the foreground.

There is little doubt that Dalí's theories and his creative involvement with this style led to a revival of interest and a reappraisal of the movement. Nothing would have pleased him more than the public reaction in 1895 to the first Art Nouveau posters of Alphonse Mucha: 'le délire . . . le délire de la laideur' ('delirium . . . delirium of the ugly').

It was nevertheless a discouraging period for Dalí. The sale of his paintings following the Goemans exhibition was not going well, which he blamed on 'the freemasonry of modern art'. Goemans had gone into bankruptcy owing him money. If the public would not buy his works, perhaps they would buy his inventions. Every day Gala would walk the

Invention of the Monsters, 1937
L'invention des monstres
Oil on canvas, 51.2 x 78.5 cm
Joseph Winterbotham Collection, Art Institute of Chicago

Dalí's interest in the Italian masters and in established aesthetic values began to have an impact on his work. To the 'great Realists', like Velázquez and Vermeer of Delft, he now added Leonardo, as in the foreground figure, recognizable as Leonardo's Madonna. The two figures seated alongside are portraits of the artist and Gala.

Hieronymus Bosch
The Garden of Earthly Delights (Triptych)
Left-hand panel: Earthly Paradise
Right-hand panel: Hell
Oil on wood, each panel 220 x 97 cm
Prado, Madrid

Palladio's Corridor of Thalia, 1937
Le corridor Thalia de Palladio
Oil on canvas, 116 x 88.5 cm
Edward James Collection, West Dean

Palladio's stage sets for the Teatro Olimpico in Vicenza, with their dramatic use of perspective, have been transformed by Dalí into human forms. He was to paint another variation on the theme, *Palladio's Corridor of Dramatic Surprise*, in 1938. Since the animate and the inanimate are indistinguishable according to his 'paranoiac' ability, Dalí sees no reason why such inanimate objects as chests, telephones and in this case architecture should not assume living forms.

streets of Paris with a portfolio of drawings for such items as transparent mannequins for shop windows, their bodies filled with water and live goldfish, bakelite furniture shaped to fit the body contours, shoes with springs to augment the pleasure of walking, artificial fingernails made of tiny reducing mirrors in which one saw oneself, dresses with false insets and anatomical padding to titillate man's erotic fantasies. Rejected as uncommercial at the time, many were to make their appearance as a result of his influence, for which he received no credit.

Dalí created many Surrealist objects for the English collector, Edward James, whom he called 'the humming-bird poet'. Among them were the Mae West sofa, made in the shape of her lips and taken from the portrait he made of her, the famous lobster telephone (p. 46) and, in James's country house in Sussex, the white grand piano in the centre of a pond, with jets of water spouting from the keyboard.

As early as 1914 Marcel Duchamp[11] had chosen 'ready-mades' and 'aided ready-mades' which could be considered the first Surrealist objects. In 1924 André Breton had suggested the making of certain objects which one only sees in dreams. In the following years Surrealism was to draw attention to various categories of objects: the found object, interpreted object, phantom object, poem object and the object with a symbolic function, conceived by Dalí as a means of representing the actions of the unconscious. These objects were intended to procure by indirect means a particular sexual emotion and, drawing on Dalí's obsessive ideas, led to the creation of such objects as *Retrospective Bust of a Woman Devoured by Ants* (destroyed 1933, reconstructed 1970), *The Aphrodisiac Jacket* (destroyed 1936), to which fifty wine glasses filled with crème de menthe and a dead fly had been attached, and the *Atmospheric Chair*, with a seat composed of bars of chocolate. On a more ambitious level were the two hundred live, edible snails crawling over a semi-nude figure in an ivy-wreathed taxi.

Dalí's shoe fetish goes back to his adolescence and appears in many paintings and objects. Schiaparelli created a hat in the form of a shoe based on an idea by him. It is an object 'most charged with realistic virtues as opposed to musical objects which I have always tried to represent as demolished, crushed, soft-cellos of rotten meat . . .'

The Surrealist object, Dalí maintained, completely discredited the dream period of Surrealism, and the meaningless writing dictated by the unconscious. He saw the object as a new reality, useless from a practical point of view but 'created wholly for the purpose of materializing in a fetishist way, with the maximum of tangible reality, ideas and fantasies of a delirious character'. People would no longer face the limitations of only talking about their manias and phobias, 'but could now touch them, manipulate and operate them with their own hands'.

He also planned a number of bread objects. 'Not,' he maintained, 'precisely intended for the succour and sustenance of large families. My

Apparition of Face and Fruit-Dish on a Beach, 1938
Apparition d'un visage et d'un compotier sur une plage
Oil on canvas, 114 x 143.8 cm
E.G. and M.C. Sumner Collections, Wadsworth Atheneum, Hartford (Connecticut)

The multiple image is revealed in a sequence of subjects. The base of the dish is also the back view of his nurse of the Rosas series, which in turn also becomes a face. The dog's head is part of the beach, its back composed of fruit. Dalí wrote: 'The double image may be extended, continuing the paranoiac advance, and then the presence of another dominant idea is enough to make a third image appear, and so on, until there is a number of images limited only by the mind's degree of paranoiac capacity.'

bread was a ferociously anti-humanitarian bread, it was the bread of the revenge of imaginative luxury on the utilitarianism of the rational practical world . . .' It was to be aristocratic, paranoiac, paralysing and phenomenal. One idea in truly typical Dalí style was to bake a loaf fifteen metres long, which was then to be placed, wrapped in newspaper, in the gardens of the Palais Royal. The public reaction and speculation was then to be reported in detail. And next day a loaf twenty metres long would be found in the courtyard of Versailles, to be followed by thirty-metre loaves appearing simultaneously in the public squares of various capitals throughout Europe.

For the first New York World Fair in 1939 Dalí's *Dream of Venus* involved seventeen live mermaids in a water-filled tank: some milked an underwater cow, others played pianos or answered telephones. Obeying only the laws of chance or of psychological necessity, such objects established a canon of the unexpected, lending coherence to a dream world which identified itself with a new exciting and poetic experience. They demonstrated the validity of Lautréamont's contention that poetry can be made by anybody and everybody.

Dalí's ceaseless use of all aspects of Surrealist activity – his critical writing, painting, his objects and poetry – were all essential contributions to the vitality of the movement. His obsession with all aspects of visual phenomena and his fascination with giving life to the inanimate and seeking out hidden biological meanings were the foundation of his way of seeing the word: 'a Renaissance man converted to psychoanalysis', according to Sarane Alexandrian.[12]

Only in a few instances did Dalí offer any explanation as to the meaning of his paintings. In *Conquest of the Irrational* he wrote: 'The fact that I myself, at the moment of painting, do not understand my own pictures does not mean that these pictures have no meaning; on the contrary, their meaning is so profound, complex, coherent and involuntary that it escapes the most simple analysis of logical intuition. To describe my pictures in everyday language, to explain them, it is necessary to submit them to special analyses, and preferably with the most ambitiously objective scientific rigour possible. A explanation arises *a posteriori* once the picture already exists as a phenomenon.' The disquieting limp watches in *The Persistence of Memory* (p. 25) came into being as a result of eating Camembert cheese, with its particular softness. 'You may be sure that the famous soft watches are nothing else than the tender, extravagant, solitary, paranoiac-critical Camembert of time and space.' Marcel Jean[13] gives a more illuminating explanation. 'The word *montre* (watch) is a word-image with a double meaning: in French, it is the imperative of the verb *montrer* (to show) and the name of the apparatus *montrant* (showing) the time. But there is a very common childhood experience: the doctor asks the sick child to *montrer sa langue* (show his tongue), which obviously is soft. The child, we may say, *la montre molle* (shows it soft,

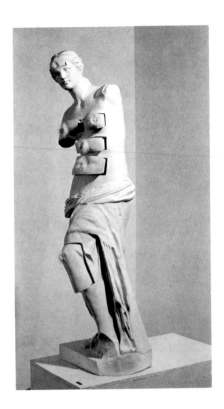

Venus de Milo with Drawers, 1936/64
Venus de Milo aux Tiroirs
Painted bronze, 98 x 32.5 x 34 cm
Private collection

Spain, 1938
Espagne
Oil on canvas, 91.8 x 60.2 cm
Boymans-van-Beuningen Museum, Rotterdam

Dalí's use of the multiple image is a genuine *tour de force*. The equestrian battle in the distance, influenced by Leonardo, is so arranged as to form the face of the woman leaning on the chest in the foreground.

with the double sense that in French this phrase can also mean 'the soft watch'). The irrational and even anguished nature of this act for the child, in view of the circumstances, could certainly constitute an experience capable of leaving profound impressions in the psyche. Here, then, is a most concrete origin for the image of the soft watches, an origin founded in an authentic childhood memory, which seems to be confirmed by the titles of the picture...' Bought by the American gallery owner Julien Levy, it was sold and resold until it was finally hung in the Museum of Modern Art, New York. It was to achieve such popular success that reproductions were even used to attract custom to furniture stores, greengrocers', and so forth.

A few years later he was to paint *The Spectre of Sex Appeal* (1931) with his explanation 'of having predicted in 1928, at the height of the cult for functional and practical anatomy, in the midst of the most shocking scepticism, the imminence of the round and salivary muscles of Mae West, viscous and terrible with hidden biological meanings. Today I announce that all the new sexual allure of women will come from the possible utilization of their capacities and resources as ghosts, that is to say, their possible dissociation, their charnel and luminous decomposition.' Now women with sex appeal would have detachable portions of their anatomy, which they could hand round for admiration. It seems unlikely that this painting is the result of a hypnotic trance or hallucination so much as an attempt, in clear consciousness, to realize one of his inspired ideas. It is conceived in brilliant colours, because he wanted it to be 'more beautiful and terrifying than the white truffle of death: a rainbow'. The image of the crutches that support the spectre, and appear in many later paintings, began when he was a child staying with Señor Pitchot. Dalí sees the crutch fetish in two ways: firstly sociologically, for 'a wealthy but weak society in need of support; secondly he sees in the shape of the crutch the significance of life and death – a support for his imagined feeling of inadequacy. The monstrous bodiless head of *Sleep* (pp. 58/59) is propped up with innumerable crutches, not only raising it off the ground but holding its features – lips, nose and eyes. He speaks of them as 'wooden supports derived from Cartesian philosophy. Generally used as a support for the tenderness of soft structure.'

By 1934 Dalí had directed his attention to what he was to call 'instantaneous' figures, possibly inspired by the particular effect of sunlight that is found on the beach at Rosas, situated a few miles from Figueras, although in his memoirs he talks of painting a few apparently very normal paintings, 'inspired by the congealed and minute enigma of certain snapshots, to which I added a Dalínian touch of Meissonier...' The ostensible subject matter could certainly have been released by seeing old snapshots of his childhood and memories of being with his nurse on the beach. These figures are, possibly, phantoms, sublimated versions of what Freud called 'the nocturnal visitors attired in nightdresses, who awoke the child

Shirley Temple, the Youngest Sacred Monster of the Cinema of Her Times, 1938
Shirley Temple, le plus jeune monstre sacré du cinéma de son temps
Gouache, pastel and collage on card, 75 x 100 cm
Boymans-van-Beuningen Museum, Rotterdam

to put him on the chamberpot so that he should not wet the bed, or who lifted the bedclothes in order to see how he held his hands in sleep'. An important feature in the works of this period is the stereoscopic effect produced by these figures against a background, as well as the complete lack of distortion in the treatment. Also discernible is a distinct move towards aesthetic values. *Paranoiac-Astral Image* (1934), *Apparition on the Beach at Rosas,* as well as *Noon* (1954), although free of his usual mannerisms and fetishist devices, achieve an apparitional effect and project a condition of apprehension that is recognized in hallucinations or in dreams. They capture a haunting premonition of a secret activity that lies midway between actual reality and the magic realm of unconscious desires. Not unrelated to the Rosas series of paintings is one of his most strikingly poetic works, *The Phantom Cart* (p. 36), in which we see that the backs of the two figures seated in the cart are really part of the buildings in the distant town. By some strange alchemy, the cart has already reached its destination while it is still some way off.

On the occasion of the Surrealist exhibition at the Galerie Colle in 1933, Dalí had proposed a catalogue preface praising the art of Meissonier, a popular academic of the 19th century, for his 'irrational exactness'. Opposition among the Surrealists was unanimous. They saw little

reason to acknowledge such a painter as a model of Surrealism. More disquieting was Dalí's interest in Nazism and Hitler's rise to power in Germany.[14] A 'Hitlerian nurse' had made its appearance in certain works, while in *The Enigma of William Tell* (p. 37) a portrait of Lenin appeared, without any trousers and with an extended buttock supported by a crutch. It paid a very different kind of homage from *Six Apparitions of Lenin on a Piano* (p. 27), painted in the previous year. *Six Apparitions*, for all its complex imagery, could be taken as a sign of Dalí's sympathy with Surrealism's political leanings. Understandably, though, such works by the Surrealists were not likely to meet with the Communists' approval, who believed in a Social Realist art, and this soon led to a break between the groups, with the formation of an 'Association of Revolutionary Writers and Artists' by the Surrealists, which Dalí refused to join.

In the political climate of the time, with Surrealism taking a more positive attitude against the forces of capitalism, changing *La Révolution Surréaliste* to *Le Surréalisme au Service de la Révolution* ('Surrealism in the Service of the Revolution'), Dalí's uneasy relationship with the movement, following the success of his first exhibition in New York at the Julien Levy Gallery, which had identified him as the only authentic voice of Surrealism, along with his growing interest in the aristocracy, monar-

Slave Market with Invisible Bust of Voltaire, 1940
Marché d'esclaves avec apparition du buste invisible de Voltaire
Oil on canvas, 46.3 x 65.5 cm
Collection of
Mr and Mrs A. Reynolds Morse,
Salvador Dalí Museum,
St. Petersburg, Florida

Voltaire's face appears in a number of works. Here it will be recognized in the two figures dressed in black, whose faces go to form the eyes of Voltaire. The area of sky seen through the irregular arch behind them forms the head.

Impressions of Africa, 1938
Impressions d'Afrique
Oil on canvas, 91.5 x 117.5 cm
Boymans-van-Beuningen Museum,
Rotterdam

'Africa must account for something in
my work, since without having been
there I remember so much about it!'
Dalí had certainly read Raymond
Roussel's *Impressions of Africa*,
which are entirely imaginary, and
which he said had been inspired by
some opera glasses with the bazaar of
Cairo painted on one lens and the
bazaar of Luxor on the other. The
brushwork shows the influence of
Velázquez. The figure at the easel is a
self-portrait and a number of double
images are evident in the background.

chy and Catholicism, led to a confrontation with the Surrealists at a
meeting in André Breton's house.

Accounts of what took place at this meeting vary. Some say he was
officially expelled, others that he was being censured for the wilder
eccentricities. Dalí turned up with a thermometer in his mouth, pretend-
ing to have 'flu. As the discussion became more heated, he kept checking
his temperature, and with each attack on him proceeded to take off one of
the numerous shirts he was wearing until, naked to the waist, he threw
himself at Breton's feet.

Dalí's defence was that his obsession with Hitler was purely paranoid
and apolitical, and he would probably be one of the first to be done away
with as a degenerate, if Europe was conquered. Not all the Surrealists
were unanimous in their opposition, and Dalí succeeded so well in creat-
ing an atmosphere of confusion and hysteria that the affair eventually
petered out. Although Dalí no longer attended the meetings, he was still
invited to contribute to the group's exhibitions, including the controver-
sial portrait of Lenin, which was shown at the Galerie Bonjean in 1934.

It was nevertheless the first sign, which Breton had already detected
when he wrote the introduction to Dalí's first Paris exhibition. But 'the
sound of Dalí's admirable voice' was to last only a few more years. In the
meanwhile he continued to enrich the movement with his research.

Between 1933 and 1936, Dalí applied his mental and creative powers to
a number of inspirational sources, as well as making literary contributions
to *Minotaure*, and to *Cahiers d'Art* for which he wrote an article on
Surrealist objects. He began to explore various skeletal and cephalic
deformations, in which figures take on grotesquely deformed growths.
*Average Atmospherocephalic Bureaucrat in the Act of Milking a Cranial
Harp (p. 35), Myself at the Age of Ten when I was the Grasshopper Child*
(1933), as well as *Meditation on the Harp* (1932–34), are typical examples
of his clinical imagination, made all the more disturbing because of our
knowledge that certain people really are victims of such disfigurations.

It was not difficult to see in the slightly ridiculous figure, without
trousers, in the act of milking the soft monstrosity, a clearly masturbatory
image, while *Meditation on the Harp* draws on the devout image of the
man in Millet's *Angelus*, but here he is being embraced by a voluptuous
nude as he hides an erection behind his hat.

In only one instance, inspired by these deformations, *Soft Construction
with Boiled Beans: Premonition of Civil War*, which was painted in 1936,
did Dalí offer some explanation of his thoughts: 'I showed a vast human
body breaking out into monstrous excrescences of arms and legs tearing
at one another in a delirium of autostrangulation. As a background to this
architecture of frenzied flesh devoured by a narcissistic and biological
cataclysm, I painted a geological landscape, that had been uselessly
revolutionized for thousands of years, congealed in its "normal course".
The soft structure of that great mass of flesh in civil war I embellished with

Geopolitical Child Watching the Birth of the New Man, 1943
Enfant géopolitique observant la naissance de l'homme nouveau
Oil on canvas, 45.7 x 52 cm
Collection of
Mr and Mrs A. Reynolds Morse,
Salvador Dalí Museum,
St. Petersburg, Florida

Dalí's decision to become classical and to 'paint pictures uniquely consecrated to the architecture of the Renaissance and the exact sciences' was made in 1941, and a growing academicism in his technique became noticeable.

Pages 74/75:
Portrait of Mrs Isabel Styler-Tas, 1945
Portrait de Mrs. Isabel Styler-Tas
Oil on canvas, 65.5 x 86 cm
National Gallery, West Berlin

a few boiled beans, for one could not imagine swallowing all that unconscious meat without the presence (however uninspiring) of some mealy and melancholy vegetable.'

Another approximation of his obsession with elongated growths supported by a crutch is *The Javanese Mannequin* (1934), with its delicately wrought skeletal body.

Among the figures of rhetoric, there is one known as catachresis, by which the imagination supplies a known word to partially describe a new object – for instance, we speak of the foot of a table, or the arm of a windmill, taking from two different objects the means to create a third one. The Oxford *Shorter English Dictionary* gives as an example, 'Lakes by the figure catachresis called seas'. Used in a visual sense, they could be described as lyrical relations, when the outline of a hill and a reclining nude are interchangeable. Less familiar among Dalí's works is a small painting entitled *Skull with its Lyrical Appendage Leaning on a Night Table which ought to be the Temperature of a Cardinal's Nest* (p. 34), showing a liquefying piano, its black and white keyboard stretched in such a manner that the keys metamorphose into the teeth of an adjoining skull. In a more restrained vein is *Nostalgic Echo* (1935), in which the outline of the young girl skipping is repeated in the shape of the bell in the tower and in the keyhole in the chest, while the shape of the wall in the foreground is repeated in the bell tower itself. Dalí's debt to de Chirico is again recognisable in the girl skipping and the shadow of an unseen presence. It is a direct allusion to the most marvellous of de Chirico's paintings, *The Mystery and Melancholy of a Street*. The reference is further strengthened by its stillness, the feeling that time itself is frozen, with everything steeped in a strange melancholy.

It was not until 1931 that the first important exhibition of Surrealism was to take place outside France. An American show was quickly followed by Dalí's solo exhibition in Barcelona. Then E. L. T. Mesens initiated another group show in Brussels in 1934. From then onwards Surrealist exhibitions became frequent – Copenhagen, Prague, Tokyo, Tenerife, Holland – and groups were formed in some fifteen countries. In June 1936 a large international exhibition was opened in the New Burlington Galleries, London. Organized by Roland Penrose, with the collaboration of the French and Belgian groups, it brought together pictures, objects, drawings, collages, and sculptures, and included African and American primitive objects as well as children's drawings. Dalí was represented by twelve works, including the *Retrospective Bust of a Woman* and *Aphrodisiac Jacket*.

During the opening, a young woman wandered through the gallery in a white gown, her head and face covered with roses on which rested live ladybirds. She wore long black surgical gloves and carried a model of a human leg in one hand and a raw piece of beef in the other.[15] The exhibition was opened by André Breton, dressed in green, smoking a

green pipe, accompanied by his wife with long green hair. During the exhibition Dalí gave a lecture in a diving suit, rented by Lord Berners for the occasion. When he was asked to specify the depth of the descent, he replied that Mr Dalí was going to descend to the unconscious. In that case, the suppliers assured him, they would supply a special helmet. Dalí appeared in the suit, decorated with plasticine hands, a radiator cap on top of the helmet, a dagger in the belt and holding two Russian wolf-hounds on leads. After delivering his lecture, quite inaudibly, from inside the helmet, Dalí, dripping with perspiration and nearly suffocating from lack of air, gestured wildly to have the helmet removed, only to discover that the mechanic had locked the bolts so securely that no one could remove it at first.

The end of that year saw a number of works, among which was the remarkable painting *Autumn Cannibalism* (p. 55), in which a liquefying figure spreads over a chest, as it eats itself with a knife and fork. One of Dalí's great contributions was to show the chaotic background to the work of art; mitigated by aesthetic control, his pictures would not be what

Apotheosis of Homer, 1944/45
Apothéose d'Homère
Oil on canvas, 64 x 119 cm
Staatsgalerie moderner Kunst,
Munich

Dalí had now become fascinated with themes of Christianity as well as discoveries in physics. About this work he said, 'Detailed narration of the world of the blind'. The work was to signify the end of his Surrealist career.

they are, and while much of his work might be considered external documentation, *Autumn Cannibalism* is a triumph of imagination. It is as though he had translated all the desires of humanity into flesh and not as usual into form.

It was two years later, in London, that Dalí realized one of his greatest ambitions, to meet Sigmund Freud, made possible with the help of Stefan Zweig. While crossing the yard on the day of the meeting, Dalí reported, 'I saw a bicycle leaning against the wall, and on the saddle, attached by a string, was a red rubber hot-water bottle, which looked full of water and on the back of the hot-water bottle walked a snail.'[16]

Freud, then seriously ill, is reported to have made only two remarks: 'In classic paintings, I look for the sub-conscious; in a Surrealist painting, for the conscious.' As his guests left, he turned to Zweig, saying: 'I have never seen a more perfect specimen of a Spaniard. What a fanatic.' Dalí was later to claim that Freud's pronouncement on Surrealist painting was a death sentence for Surrealist doctrine. From now on it was to be not experimentation but tradition, not revolution but renaissance.

The Madonna of Port Lligat, 1950
La Madone de Port Lligat
Oil on canvas, 144 x 96 cm
Lady Beaverbrook Collection,
Canada

Dalí's preoccupation with a more con-scious objectivity and also Roman Catholicism were the inspiration for the iconography of this work, about which he has said: 'The weaning of furniture nourishment made sacred: instead of a hole in my nurse's back, a tabernacle containing the divine bread open in the body of Jesus.'

Dalí's patron, Edward James, bought many of his works during that period, and he was a frequent guest at James's house. At that time his English was practically non-existent, which could account for the mis-understanding that arose upon hearing someone talk of 'a chest of draw-ers'. Interpreting this quite literally, Dalí in *Anthropomorphic Cabinet* (pp. 44/45) as well as a number of drawings, was to show a reclining woman out of whose chest appeared numerous half-open drawers. The idea could have been supplemented by an awareness of the 17th-century drawings of Bracelli, showing the human figure constructed of such items as boxes, tennis rackets and bell towers.

Few artists have shown their contempt for the machine so strongly as Dalí. Contemporary industrial products are invariably treated with sav-age disregard for their natural properties, either by transforming them into living forms, or by reducing them to the fury of disintegration. The motor car which appears in a number of his works never looks as though it will run, and in *Paranoiac-Critical Solitude* (p. 47) it has been excavated, fossil-like, from the rock. 'Machines are doomed to crumble and rust,' he claimed. Mechanical brains like television kill imagination and the spirit of man. Why were people so incapable of fantasy? Why, for instance, didn't manufacturers of toilets hide a bomb in the flush, to detonate when politicians pulled the cord? Why, when ordering lobster, didn't one get a cooked telephone? Dalí's hatred of mass-production led him to consider an automobile in the absurd act of gestation, as in *Debris of an Auto-mobile Giving Birth to a Blind Horse Biting a Telephone* (1938).

At some point during Dalí's stay in England, he discovered the paint-ings of the Pre-Raphaelite Brotherhood, in whose works he found 'para-noiac' evidence. Their very literary subject matter and highly elaborated symbolism, combined with an obsessional attention to detail, were all qualities that appealed to Dalí's own predilection. When he wrote 'Le surréalisme spectral de l'éternal féminin pré-raphaelite' ('The spectral surrealism of eternal Pre-Raphaelite femininity'), it was not an attempt to justify the movement aesthetically, but to explore the hidden meaning behind the outward appearance. Breton had made clear the Surrealist's distrust of art criticism. He saw it as 'a complete failure' because the critic describes the form rather than the content. The true value of any work was its ability, not to represent, but to prefigure. Breton suggested the search for a new beauty that would be acceptable to our time. 'Beauty will be convulsive',[17] he insisted, and expressed his complete lack of interest in works of art that did not produce 'a state of physical disturbance characterized by the sensation of a wind brushing across my forehead and causing me to really shiver', a sensation he relates to erotic pleasure. Dalí's paranoiac method, extended to his writings, contributed to the revelatory nature of that which exists beneath the surface reality.

Unlike his other literary ventures into the significance of Millet's *Angelus*, the legend of William Tell and Art Nouveau, Dalí's meditations

on the Pre-Raphaelites left no visible traces in his art. Possibly he merely wished to illustrate his enthusiasm for all that ran counter to the prevailing fashion of the times and the appeal to 'the bad taste of the age' that Breton spoke of. It was not until 1944, in the painting *Tristan as Christ,* that Dalí seems to have been partially inspired by Burne-Jones, in the detail of the jewelled breastplate, the semi-transparent veil and preposterous pose of the figure which only revealed the dubious nature of his growing academicism.

Between 1937 and 1939, Dalí made three visits to Italy. Rome, 'Catholic in essence and in substance', he found was being destroyed under Mussolini's modernization, architecturally conceived 'by the brain of one of those lamentable organizers of international exhibitions'. He joined Edward James at Amalfi, where he found inspiration for his Wagnerian ballet and spent two months on *Impressions of Africa* (p. 71) in which the treatment owes more to Velázquez than to any Italian master. The Munich crisis of 1938 prompted a move to Monte Carlo and another painting, *The Enigma of Hitler,* based on dreams brought on by the events of Munich. This picture appeared to him 'to be charged with a prophetic value, as announcing the mediaeval period which was going to cast its shadow over Europe'. Chamberlain's umbrella appeared in this painting in a sinister aspect, identified with the bat, and 'affected me as extremely anguishing at the very time I was painting it . . .'

In 1939 he made a second journey to America for his exhibition at the Julien Levy Gallery. New York, 'an immense Gothic Roquefort cheese', was already familiar with this Paris Surrealist. His two previous exhibitions, lectures at the Museum of Modern Art, as well as the illustrations of the city made for the *American Weekly* in a four-page spread, left little doubt of his growing popularity with the American public. *Time* magazine put him on the cover, and Dalí images soon appeared everywhere. Bonwit-Teller in Fifth Avenue invited him to make a window display. The theme was to be Night and Day.

Night was symbolized by a bed with a canopy consisting of a buffalo clutching a bloody pigeon in its mouth. The legs of the bed were the four feet of the animal. Black bedsheets were covered with burn marks, and a wax mannequin of the 1900 vintage, covered in dust and cobwebs, lay across the bed with her head resting on artificial live coals. Day showed another mannequin climbing into an ermine-lined bath filled with water, while a pair of wax arms held a mirror before her. Flowers grew out of the floor and surrounding furniture.

The following day Dalí discovered that the decor had been altered, his wax mannequins replaced by conventional ones and the bed removed. Furious, Dalí entered the display window and tried to upturn the bath of water, only to slip and project the tub through the plate glass window into the watching crowd outside. Arrested by the police, he was taken before a magistrate and given a suspended sentence.

Christ of St John of the Cross, 1951
Christ de Saint Jean de la Croix
Oil on canvas, 205 x 116 cm
Glasgow Art Gallery and Museum, Glasgow

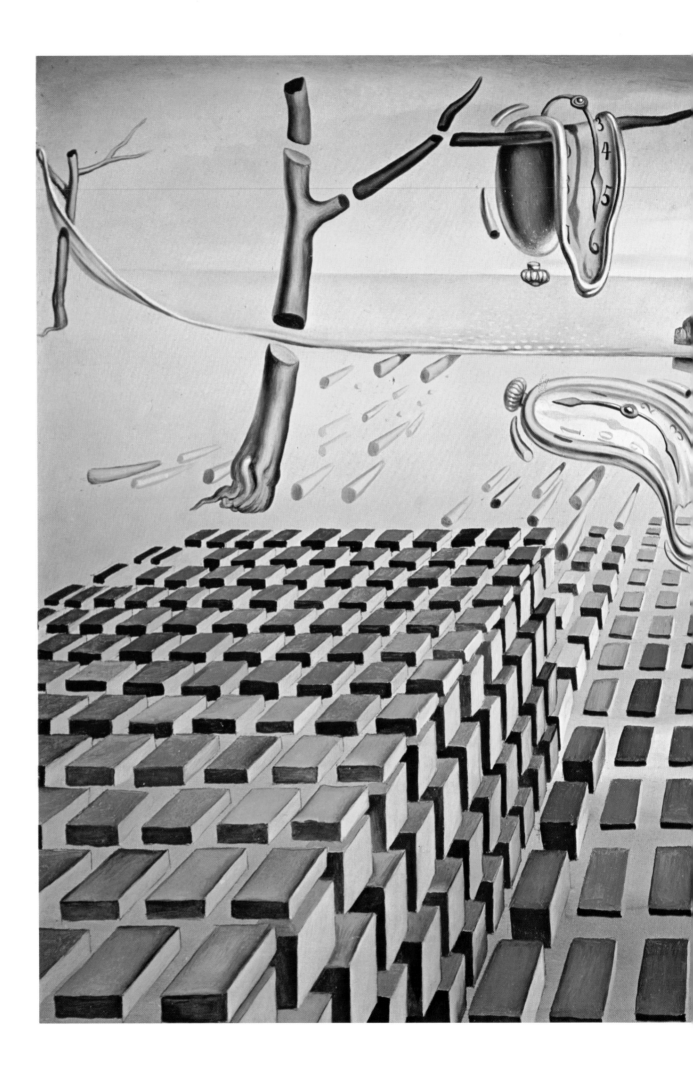

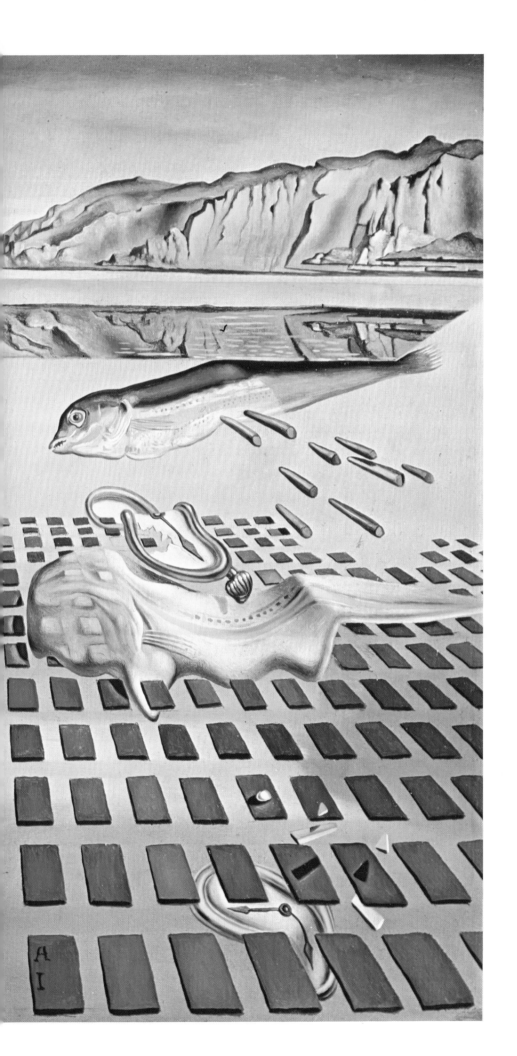

The Disintegration of the Persistence of Memory, 1952/54
Desintégration de la persistance de la mémoire
Oil on canvas, 25.5 x 33 cm
Collection of
Mr and Mrs A. Reynolds Morse,
Salvador Dalí Museum,
St. Petersburg, Florida

The full title of this work is *The Chromosomes of a Highly Coloured Fish's Eye Starting the Harmonious Disintegration of the Persistence of Memory*. A number of compositional changes have been introduced into this work, which is based on the 1931 *Persistence of Memory* (p. 25). The watch covered in ants has disappeared. The surface of the sea hangs sheet-like from the branch of a tree, and a fish now lies on what was a deserted beach. 'After twenty years of complete immobility,' said Dalí, 'the soft watches distintegrate dynamically . . .'

Young Virgin Autosodomized by her Own Chastity, 1954
Jeune vierge autosodomisée par les cornes de sa propre chasteté
Oil on canvas, 40.5 x 30.5 cm
Playboy Collection, Los Angeles

Dalí commented on the picture: 'The horn of the rhinoceros, at one time the uniceros, is in reality the horn of the legendary unicorn, the symbol of chastity. A young virgin can rely on it, or play moral games with it, as well as she would have done in the days of courtly love.'

No less disastrous from Dalí's point of view was his sideshow for the New York World Fair, called 'Dalí's Dream of Venus'. He soon discovered that all the corporation wanted was his name, completely ingnoring his ideas. Thoroughly disgusted, he sat down and wrote a manifesto, *Declaration of Independence of the Imagination and of the Rights of Man to his own Madness*. Before the 'Dream' was finished he left for France. The means Dalí cynically used to publicize himself, his endorsement of Franco in Spain and the growing academicism of his work had not passed unnoticed by the Surrealists, who rightly considered that he was bringing discredit to the ideas of Surrealism. This time the decision was unanimous: he was to be completely ignored by the movement. Dalí had always insisted that he took Surrealism literally, and that he neglected nothing to become the 'integral Surrealist', the logical upshot of which was his 'paranoiac-critical activity'. With equal determination he intended to 'become its leader as soon as possible', and to be recognized as the only authentic Surrealist. This was the attitude least calculated to identify him with a movement that had, since its inception, proclaimed a community of aims and had no wish to see Surrealism diminished by a wholehearted endorsement of his reactionary technique.

The advent of war brought a temporary truce to the Dalí affair. After immense difficulties, some of the French Surrealists succeeded in reaching America. Man Ray and Nicolas Calas had arrived earlier and were soon joined by Tanguy, Masson, Matta, Duchamp, Seligmann and Breton. After moving to Spain, then Lisbon, Dalí and Gala reached New York with the help of their friend, Caresse Crosby.[18] Recovering from their adventures at the country home of the Crosbys, Dalí began writing his autobiography, widening his aesthetic interests and strengthening the ties with the Italian tradition. The Divine Proportion or, as Plato called it, the 'Golden Section' now received his attention, a principle he incorporated in the *Family of Marsupial Centaurs* (1940), with its rigid diagonals dividing the composition into four equal triangles. Here Dalí's hand is fully engaged by his conscious mind to achieve the Platonic ideal. It was to mark his reaction against the eloquence of his earlier works, in which revelation and discovery was the profound aim, and in which his masterly technique was used as a means and not as an end.

A return to classicism demanded a more conscious objectivity and a study of the pictorial principles used by Renaissance artists. Geometry, mathematics, anatomy and perspective now received the same fanatical enthusiasm that earlier he had reserved for the interrogation of the unconscious as a springboard for artistic inspiration. Both *Leda* (1949) and *The Madonna of Fort Lligat* (p. 79) are based on the Pythagorean pentagram, while the golden rectangle dominates *The Sacrament of the Last Supper* (p. 86). For Dalí it meant 'integration, synthesis, cosmogony, faith'. He rejected his past as 'fragmentation, experimentation, scepticism'. With it all came an increased belief in the Catholic hierarchy and in

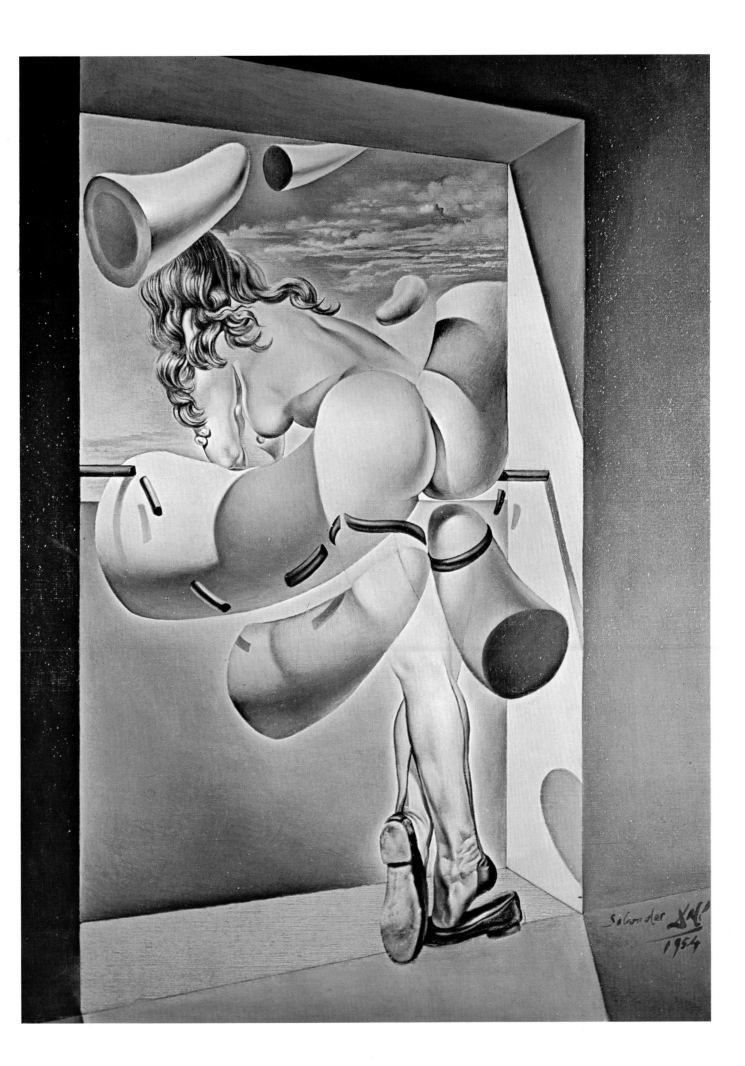

the monarchy. No wonder, then, that we find him seeking the Pope's approval of one of his paintings. His hope for the future was clearly stated: 'a religious renaissance based on a progressive form of Catholicism'. Despite such views, and there are many on the subject, he believed he was the only true Surrealist. By means of such mental gymnastics did Dalí seek to integrate Surrealism into the very aesthetic continuum which it had always been out to destroy.

During the war years in America, his flair for showmanship and publicity stunts, always good for newspaper headlines, made him a household name to millions, who confused his money-making clowning with Surrealism. His success may afford an explanation of Dalí's refusal to distinguish painting from other, minor arts and other aspects of aesthetics.

During the early 1940s he painted several portraits of the rich and famous, and it was probably his long association with Jack Warner, the Hollywood producer, in the five years it took to complete his portrait, that led to Dalí's revived interest in the film as a medium. Hitchcock's *Spellbound*, based on the novel *The House of Mr Edwards*, had dream sequences conceived by Dalí. His own *Wheelbarrow of Flesh* (quoted by Fleur Cowles) remained unfilmed; in it a paranoiac woman falls in love with a wheelbarrow. It contains such scenes as swans stuffed with explosives blowing up, rhinoceroses climbing into the Trevi fountain in Rome, hundreds of priests on bicycles carrying posters of Malenkov, and

The Sacrament of the Last Supper, 1955
La cène
Oil on canvas, 167 x 268 cm
Chester Dale Collection, National Gallery of Art, Washington D.C.

Dalí based his work on the number 12: 12 hours of the day, 12 months of the year, 12 pentagons of the dodecahedron, 12 signs of the Zodiac, 12 Apostles around Christ. 'The Communion must be symmetrical,' he insisted.

a shaven-headed woman, balancing an omelette on her head, standing in the middle of a lake. He wrote the screenplay, designed scenery and costumes for two ballets, designed jewellery in collaboration with the Duke di Verdura, and devoted time to writing over thirty books. His activity also touched on advertising, fashions for Chanel and Schiaparelli, and lecture tours around the US circuit.

In the meantime, the Surrealists were becoming established in New York. Under Charles Henri Ford, the *View* devoted a number of issues to Surrealism, including an attack on Dalí by Nicholas Calas, titled 'I say his flies are ersatz'.[19] In 1942 they started their own review, *VVV*. Dalí was to remain isolated from the group's activity, who now referred to him as 'Avida Dollars' ('greedy dollars'), an anagram coined by Breton, or chose only to reproduce one of his advertisements for Schiaparelli stockings. Unperturbed, Dalí continued his own career as a 'completely deviant Surrealist' and set about cornering the religious market. The galactic forms revealed in the whorls of cauliflowers and the nuclear mysticism in the spiral of the rhinoceros horn were now given significance in his new works. In 1947 the Loew-Lewin film company organized a competition for a painting of *The Temptation of St Anthony* to be used in their film *The*

Galacidalacidesoxyribonucleidacid, 1963
Galacidalacidesoxyribonucleidacid
Oil on canvas, 305 x 345 cm
New England Merchants National Bank, Boston (Massachusetts)

The molecular structures that were to appear in a number of works of this period are in this case those of desoxyribonucleic acid (DNA).

Pages 88/89:
The Railway Station at Perpignan, 1965
La gare de Perpignan
Oil on canvas, 295 x 406 cm
Museum Ludwig, Cologne

Nude Figures in the Wild Landscape of Cape Creus, 1970
Cap Creus con desnudos
Oil on copper, 39 x 49 cm
Private collection

Nude, 1974
Desnudo de Calcomania
Various elements on card
Private collection
Never previously published

Private Affairs of Bel Ami. From the eleven works submitted, five of which were by Surrealists, the jury chose the Max Ernst. Dalí's contribution, which was less conventional, was by far the most outstanding. He wrote about it: 'The hermit sees in the clouds the paranoid hallucinations of his temptation. The elephants carry on their backs erotic fountains, obelisks, churches, mausoleums. Elephants stride on the almost invisible legs of the spiders of desire. With outstretched arm, the saint bears his cross to exorcize the vision.' More revealing are the complex feelings that the picture betrays when one considers how ineffectual the cross appears against the advancing horde.

During Dalí's Classical period he fluctuated both in purpose and in style. The liaison between Freud and Catholicism proposed a new reality, dependent in part on a laborious reconstruction of the past and the incongruities from the subconscious. At the same time, conspicuous technical changes became noticeable in Dalí's art, characterized by a more romantic handling of colour and a softening of forms that previously had been sharply defined. Also it was clear that he had no intention of relinquishing his personal symbols, which often make their appearance in

Baisantoje Empordanes, 1978
Oil on copper
Enrique Sabater Collection

Dalí's long-lasting interest in the Mannerist and Baroque traditions is noticeable in this painting, with its love of impasto and frenzied brush-work.

quite unlikely works. These early images once had significance but had now become something of a mannerism.

From 1960 Dalí continued to extend his new mysticism. His mental and visual resources were brought to bear on the automatism of Abstract Expressionism, and he experimented with shooting lead bullets filled with ink at a lithographic stone for his illustrations to *Don Quixote*. Molecular structures give a new spatial dimension to paintings like *Tuna Fishing* (1966/67), *The Ascension of St Cecilia* and *Galacidalacidesoxyri-*

bonucleicacid (p. 87). At the same time, he launched the concept of a cosmic Dalí,[20] rationally painting his re-found reality – 'the saviour of modern painting'. For half the year, Dalí then retired to his beloved Port Lligat in Spain, where he lived like an ascetic, drawing strength from the isolation and peace of the surroundings. For, as he assured us, 'it is difficult to hold the world's interest for more than half an hour at a time. I myself have done so successfully every day for twenty years'. He went on doing so till the end of his life. And still the fascination is undiminished.

Salvador Dalí:

1904 Born 11th May at Figueras, Catalonia, Spain.

1914–18 Educated at the Academy of the Brothers of the Marist Order in Figueras.

1918–19 Experimented with Impressionism under the influence of Ramón Pitchot.

1920 Influenced by Italian Futurists after seeing catalogues and manifestoes from Paris.

1921 Became a pupil at the School of Painting, Sculpture and Drawing in Madrid. Met Luis Buñuel, Federico García Lorca and Pedro Garfias. Influenced by Cubism and Juan Gris.

1922 Rejected Cubism and adopted the tenets of the 'Metaphysical School' of paintings which, under the guidance of Giorgio de Chirico and Carlo Carrà, explored the world of inner perception and experience. Suspended for a year from the School for rebellion.

1924 Imprisoned in Gerona for supposed political activity. Illustrated *Les Bruixes de Llers* by Carles Fages de Climent.

1925 Returned to the School in Madrid. Studied writings of Sigmund Freud. First solo exhibition at Dalmau Gallery, Barcelona. Received praise from local art critics. First visit to Paris, where he met Picasso.

1926 Permanent expulsion from School. Second solo exhibition at Dalmau Gallery. Influenced by Cubism and Picasso.

1927–29 Contributed to *Gaseta de les Arts* .

1928 His *Ana Maria* and *Seated Girl* were his first paintings to be shown in America, at the Carnegie Institute in Pittsburg.

1929 Contributed to *Gaseta de les Arts* . Second visit to Paris where he was introduced to Breton, Eluard and other Surrealists by Miró. Painted *Illumined Pleasures* (p. 16), *The Lugubrious Game* (p. 14) and other truly Surrealist works. Joined the Surrealist group in Paris. Was visited by Breton, Magritte, Gala and Eluard. Gala stayed with Dalí. Influenced by Ernst and Miró. Several mixed-media collages. First showing of the film *Un Chien Andalou*, for

Salvador Dalí, around 1929

which Dalí and Buñuel wrote the scenario.

1929–30 Came under the influence of Art Nouveau and the architecture of Gaudí. Rediscovered de Chirico of the early period (p. 24) as well as the 16th-century fantasies of Arcimboldo. Wrote and illustrated *The Invisible Woman*, in which he explained his 'paranoiac-critical method'. Illustrated *The Immaculate Conception* by André Breton and Paul Eluard. Collaborated with Buñuel on the film *L'Age d'Or* (The Golden Age, p. 20), shown in the same year at Studio 28, Paris, for the first time. In the ensuing fracas paintings by Ernst, Miró, Dalí, Tanguy and Man Ray were destroyed.

1930–33 Wrote *L'Amour de la Mémoire* and contributed to the periodical *Le Surréalisme au service de la révolution* (Surrealism in the Service of the Revolution). Applied his paranoiac-critical method to the legend of William Tell (p. 37), and the use of double image in many

paintings. Fascinated by Vermeer's *The Artist in his Studio*.

1930–39 Illustrated the Second Manifesto of Surrealism, *Le Révolver à Cheveux Blancs* by Breton, *Grains et Issues* by Tristan Tzara, *Cours Natural* by Paul Eluard, *Les Chants de Maldoror* by Isadore Ducasses (Comte de Lautréamont). Published an album with six photographs of paintings.

1931 Paintings and drawings for the *New Surrealism* exhibition at the Wadsworth Atheneum, Hartford, Connecticut.

1932 Wrote the book *Babaouo*, which included an essay on William Tell and a cinema critique. Exhibitions at the Julien Levy Gallery, N.Y.

1933 First solo exhibition at the Julien Levy Gallery. Article on Millet's *Angelus* in *Minotaure*.

1934 First solo exhibition in London (Zwemmer Gallery). The Surrealists growing more and more concerned about his political pronouncements. Praise of Hitler and monarchist leanings led to official reprimand from Group. No longer attended Surrealists' meetings. First visit to America. Illustrations of New York in *American Weekly*.

1934–37 Series of paintings influenced by the effect of light on the beach at Rosas. Hitler, Lenin, *The Angelus* and telephones influenced his iconography.

1935 Wrote *The Conquest of the Irrational*, defining his 'paranoiac-critical activity' and attacking abstract act.

1936 Exhibited at the International Surrealist Exhibition in London. Friendship with the English collector, Edward James, who formed the most representative collection of Dalí's early work.

1937 Wrote *The Metamorphosis of Narcissus*, illustrating his double-

chronology

image painting of the same name (pp. 56/57). First visit to Italy. Influenced by Palladio as well as Renaissance and Baroque paintings.

1938 Through Stefan Zweig and Edward James met Sigmund Freud in London. Made a portrait of him on blotting paper.

1939 Created a Surrealist shop window for Bonwit-Teller in New York. Arrested for smashing the window. Created *The Dream of Venus* side show for the New York World Fair. Published *Declaration of the Independence of the Imagination and of the Rights of Man to his Own Madness*. Performance of ballet entitled *Bacchanale*, with scenario and scenery by Dalí.

1940 Left France at the beginning of the war. Moved first to Spain, then to California where he remained until 1948.

1941–42 Major retrospective exhibition, Museum of Modern Art. Shown in eight cities. Established his reputation in the U.S.A. Created sets for the ballets *Labyrinth, El Cafe de Chinitas* and *Sentimental Colloquy*. Wrote his autobiography *The Secret Life of Salvador Dalí*. Began to paint portraits.

1943 Exhibition at Knoedler Gallery, New York. Completed studies for murals for the home of Helena Rubinstein. Wrote his novel *Hidden Faces*. Illustrations for *The Maze* by Maurice Sandoz; *Essays of Michel de Montaigne, As You Like It* and *The Autobiography of Benvenuto Cellini*.

1948 Returned to Port Lligat, Spain. Became classical. Illustrated *50 Secrets of Magic Craftsmanship*.

1949 First religious paintings. *The Madonna of Port Lligat* (p.79) was sanctioned by the Pope.

1951–52 Illustrations for Dante's *Divine Comedy*. Painted *Christ of St John of the Cross* (p. 81). Wrote *Manifesto Mystique* which attempts to explain his mysticism.

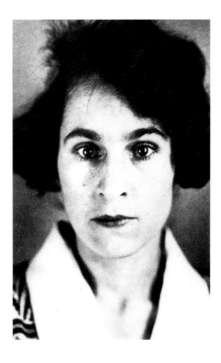

Gala, Dalí's lover, wife and muse, 1927

1954–55 Published *Dalí's Moustache* with Philippe Halsman. Retrospective in Rome. Painted *Corpus Hypercubicus* and *The Sacrament of the Last Supper* (p. 86).

1956–59 Retrospective at Knokke Le Zoute, Belgium. Painted *Santiago El Grande*, now in Beaverbrook Art Gallery, Canada. First historical painting *The Discovery of America*. Wrote *Dalí on Modern Art*.

1957 Designed a night club in Acapulco which would move and breathe. The project was never realized.

1958 Married Gala. Church wedding in Spain. Lectured at the Théâtre de l'Etoile with a 12-metre loaf of bread.

1960 Surrealists protested at his participation in the Surrealist Exhibition at the D'Arcy Galleries, New York.

1961–63 New edition of *The Secret Life of Salvador Dalí*. *Ballet de Gala* and Scarlatti's opera, *The Span-ish Lady and the Roman Cavalier*. Completed his religious painting *The Ecumenical Council*, also *The Battle of Tetuan* and *Galacidalacidesoxyribonucleidacid* (p. 87). Published *The Tragic Myth of the 'Angelus' of Millet*.

1964 Awarded one of the highest Spanish decorations, the Grand Cross of Queen Isabella of Spain.

1964–65 Major exhibition in Tokyo. Wrote *Journal of a Genius*. Illustrations for the Bible. Began producing 'three-dimensional art' and the *Bust of Dante* sculpture.

1966–73 Alain Bosquet's *Conversations with Dalí*. Illustrated a deluxe edition of *Alice in Wonderland*, published by Random House. Harry N. Abrahams Inc., New York, published *Dalí by Dalí* with illustrations chosen by the artist and grouped under separate headings – the planetarian, the molecular, the monarchical, the hallucinogenic and the futuristic Dalí.

1973 The Dalí Museum opened at his birthplace Figueras. Publication of *How to Become Dalí*.

1974 Completed the hologram *The Shepherd and the Siren* for Enrique Sabater, which includes a rare portrait of Gala.

1978 First public showing in the Teatro Museo Dalí in Figueras, of *Babaouo*, a film based on the book first written in 1932.

1979 Retrospective exhibition at the Centre Pompidou, Paris, with a unique installation *The Heroic Fun Fair*.

1980 Retrospective exhibition at the Tate Gallery, London.

1982 Created Marquis of Pubol. Gala died.

1983 Dalí withdrew to his stately home at Pubol, where he lived on his own. Last painting *The Swallow's Tail*. His state of health no longer allowed him to exert himself.

1986 Was badly burnt in a fire in his bedroom.
From then onwards Dalí spent the rest of his life serious ill and bedridden in the tower of his museum at Figueras.

1989 Dalí died at Figueras on 29th January.

[1] Dalí, Salvador, The Secret Life of Salvador Dalí, translated by Haakon M. Chevalier, revised edition, Vision Press, London 1961; © 1946, 1961 Salvador Dalí, used with permission of Dial Press, New York.

[2] Breton, André, The Manifestoes of Surrealism, Ann Arbor 1972.

[3] Introduction to the catalogue of the first Dalí exhibition, Goemans Gallery, Paris 1929.

[4] Ibid.

[5] For this purpose the Surrealists used a number of automatic processes. Decalcomania, or transfer, is a technique which was developed by Dominguez and which was later used by Max Ernst in works such as *Napoleon in the Desert*, *The Eye of Silence* and *Europe after the Rain*, which were all painted around 1937. Paalen invented fumage. Max Ernst started using frottage in 1925. This involves placing a piece of paper or canvas on an uneven surface or some object and rubbing it with a pencil or a piece of chalk. It is worth noting that once these processes had been discovered by chance, they were all subject to the artist's conscious control.

[6] Gascoyne, David, A Short Survey of Surrealism, Cobden-Sanderson, London 1935, p. 103.

[7] Cowles, Fleur, The Case of Salvador Dalí. William Heinemann, London 1959.

[8] 136 recipes by Dalí were published in Savador Dalí, Les Diners de Gala, Draeger, Paris 1973.

[9] Dalí, Salvador, Fifty Secrets of Magic Craftsmanship, Dial Press, New York 1948.

[10] From Dalí's book *The Conquest of the Irrational*, 1935.

[11] Marcel Duchamps' marginal role in the Surrealist movement is not a subject of this book. Nevertheless, the banality of his anti-art objects did form quite a significant contribution to the movement. Especially, however, his obsessive tendency to reinforce his philosophical speculations by means of written statements later secured him the attention of the abstract painters within the modern "establishment", many of whom still draw on his projects and pronouncements.

[12] Alexandrian, Saran, L'art surréaliste, Fernand Hazan, Paris 1969.

[13] Jean, Michel, Histoire de la peinture surréaliste, Editions du Seuil, Paris 1959.

[14] Although Dalí did not comment on the Spanish Civil War, his sympathies were with Franco. After the Second World War he repeatedly expressed his admiration for Hitler.

[15] In Marcel Jean's *History of Surrealist Paintings* she can be seen among the pigeons of Trafalgar Square.

Jean, Marcel, A History of Surrealist Paintings, London 1960

[16] He had already discovered earlier that Freud's skull was shaped like a snail – with a spiral brain.

[17] 'Beauty Will Be Convulsive', in *What is Surrealism*, translated by David Gascoyne, Faber & Faber, London 1936.
André Breton published this statement for the first time in: Breton, André: Nadja, Gallimard, Paris 1928.

[18] A vivid account of this time is given in Caresse Crosby's autobiography *The Passionate Years* (Dial Press, New York 1953).

[19] Calas, Nicolas, Anti-Surrealist Dalí, in View No. 6, New York, June 1941.

[20] Dalí Salvador, Dalí per Dalí, Praeger, Paris 1970.